MUSCLE CARS

MUSCLE CARS

THE MEANEST POWER ON THE ROAD

Ben Klemenzson

CRESTLINE

This edition first published in 2002 by Crestline, an imprint of
MBI Publishing Company, Galtier Plaza, Suite 200,
380 Jackson Street, St. Paul, MN 55101-3885 USA

© Salamander Books Ltd., 2002

A member of **Chrysalis** Books plc

MBI Publishing Company books are also available at discounts
in bulk quantity for industrial or sales-promotional use. For
details write to Special Sales Manager at Motorbooks
International Wholesalers & Distributors, Galtier Plaza, Suite
200, 380 Jackson Street, St. Paul, MN 55101-3885 USA.

Library of Congress Cataloging-in-Publication Data Available

ISBN 0-7603-1436-5

Designed and edited by:
FOCUS PUBLISHING, 11a St Botolph's Road, Sevenoaks,
Kent, England TN13 3AJ
Editors: Guy Croton, Vanessa Townsend
Designer: Philip Clucas MSIAD

Salamander editor: Marie Clayton
Salamander publishing director: Colin Gower

All photography by: Mike Mueller

Printed and bound in Taiwan

Contents

Introduction

Muscle Cars are a uniquely American phenomenon and, depending on whom you speak to,
they either died off in the early 1970s, or they're still here with us today—alive and kicking.
What makes a muscle car? Well, many people have their own theories and opinions, but it's
generally accepted that only a very general definition can cover the kaleidoscope of
cars which come under the broad umbrella term of "muscle car." Criteria can include a
large engine displacement and powerful brake horsepower and acceleration figures,
American origin, and some would argue, a two-door body style.
While the concept of building cars with performance buyers specifically in mind
didn't really take off until the 1960s, there can be little doubt that the popularity of racing
during the Fifties and Sixties played a large role in ensuring that manufacturers began
building these factory hot rods (or muscle cars) ready to race, straight off the showroom
floor. In this book we will be celebrating some of the milestone cars which make up the
muscle car genre, concentrating predominantly on cars from the late 1950s, 1960s,
and early 1970s. Only today can we look back at these cars and say with
certainty: "They'll never build 'em like that again!"

Left: The ultimate muscle car: a '65 Plymouth
Satellite convertible with a mighty Hemi engine.

The History of Muscle Cars

The word "muscle car" means many things to many people. Some would argue that, strictly-speaking, the orthodox definition of a muscle car is a mass-produced, mid-size, two-door, American car powered by a large V8 engine. However, as we'll see over the following pages, muscle cars have taken many different forms over the years, from full-sized behemoths to sprightly compacts, and pony cars.

For many these cars evoke memories of a glorious bygone era, when horsepower was king, cars had real character, and there really was "power for the people" down at their local car dealership. For others the word "muscle car" sums up all that went wrong with Detroit during its heydays in the 1950s, 1960s, and 1970s, seeing cars with such big engines as profligate and pointless. Indeed, there can be no denying that at the height of the muscle car wars, vehicles were often marketed solely on the basis of their brake horsepower ratings, torque output, and acceleration figures.

But to concentrate on the negative aspects of so-called muscle cars—like the fact that they "sucked gas"—is to miss the point of these exciting

Far left: Who started the whole muscle car phenomenon? Many reckon it was the Chrysler 300 which got the ball rolling back in the 1950s.

Below: It was the 1955 Chrysler C300 which introduced the world to the legendary FirePower Hemi V8 engine.

automobiles. These vehicles were automotive works of art, thoroughbred stallions of the motoring world and, even more crucially, they were products of their time, available to everyone and anyone from their local Ford, GM, or Chrysler dealerships—and all on easy finance terms!

It is almost impossible to conduct an all-encompassing, exhaustive survey of the entire muscle car era within the confines of a book of this size. Indeed, it would be difficult to cover everything accurately even within the confines of a whole series of books! Rather, we'll limit ourselves to the high

Above left: Even as the muscle car era was beginning, some of the flamboyant styling cues from the 1950s remained, such as this rather elaborate Plymouth steering wheel.

Above right: Ford offered their top gun engine in the 1962 Ford 500XL—the 405bhp Thunderbird Special 406cu in V8, which made use of three Holley two-barrel carburetors.

points of the Muscle Car era. In this brief introduction, I'll touch on the cars and phenomena that you can read about in more depth (if you feel so inclined!) later on in this book.

Chrysler Muscles In

For many people the muscle car era was kick-started by Chrysler, who introduced the Firepower or "Hemi" V8 (so-called because of its hemispherical-shaped combustion chambers), in 1951. The Hemi engine was revolutionary in that it utilized overhead valve and "V"-design rather than a side-valve, straight-eight layout, as had been the norm before the Second World War. Although Oldsmobile and Cadillac had beaten Chrysler in getting their OHV V8 engines into production three years earlier in 1948, Chrysler's V8 was an exceptional powerplant. Offering almost 200bhp (180bhp, to be precise), it was recognized as the benchmark V8 engine against which all others should be measured.

Chryslers were not considered to be particularly upmarket or prestigious cars like Cadillacs, Lincolns, or Chrysler's own prestige marque, Imperial. They were good, solid, middle-ground cars, which meant the new powerful Hemi Firepower engine was now available to a much wider selection of America's car buying public. Suddenly high performance vehicles were no longer just the preserve of the wealthy, or European sports car enthusiasts.

Below: The Dodge 426 Max Wedge was known as the Ramcharger and ranks as one of the all-time legends of drag strip folklore. Fitted in Dodge's lightweight intermediates such as the 330 or the upmarket Polara, the Ramcharger made these cars devastatingly powerful, offering well over 400bhp and enabling them to turn in scorching quarter-mile times. To many Chrysler fans the Max Wedge is an icon.

Viva the V8

The automotive press raved about Chrysler's fantastic new engine, but it wasn't until 1955, when Chevy unveiled their small-block V8, that cheap powerful V8s truly became almost commonplace, available to the ordinary American car buyer. Prior to this, V8 engines had solely been the preserve of the upper end of the car market. With Chevy's 162bhp 265cu in V8, GM had succeeded in getting V8-powered cars on the market at both ends of the automotive spectrum, first with Cadillac in 1948 and now again with Chevrolet in 1955.

Now that V8 power had been established as the standard power-train for many cars (if it was not standard, then it cost only a few dollars extra

Below: Everyone wanted to get a piece of the performance action back in the early-1960s, even Ford with their big Galaxies and Fairlanes...

Right: ...but it was Chrysler Corp who had the most success in persuading the public that their cars were really powerful and exciting to own.

Above: One of the key components to creating powerful engines in the muscle car era was multiple carburetion fuel delivery systems. Now tri-carb (three two-barrel carbs) and dual-quads (two four-barrel carbs) were available.

on the options list), it was only a matter of time before manufacturers started to compete with each other in terms of power outputs, acceleration, and engine size. Interestingly, this craze for more power and bigger engines wasn't a phenomenon limited to the higher-priced end of the car market, but one which was almost universal throughout the whole spectrum— from the cheapest Chevys and Fords, to the most expensive Cadillacs and Lincolns.

Lincoln had been doing very well with their Capri in the mid-1950s, which was earning itself the nickname the "Hot Rod Lincoln" after some exceptional performances in the Mexican road race, or Pan Americana rally. As a result of lessons learnt from these races, Lincoln bored their V8 engine out to 368cu in and increased compression to 9.0:1. These engines were rated at 285bhp and offered around 400lb ft of torque—exceptional figures back then, especially in what were traditionally thought of as "sedate" luxury cars! But these luxury cars weren't cleaning up solely on the basis of their powerful engines: the mid-1950s Lincolns (unlike their

man on the street with their small-block V8 in 1955, spotted this trend and brought out their own factory hot rod version of what was America's best selling sedan—the Impala SS. A sporty option on the popular Impala, the car was now offered with Chevrolet's new 250bhp 348cu in Turbo-Thrust V8. And if that wasn't power enough, buyers could tick the option box to substitute the four-barrel carburetor for a row of three two-barrel carbs.

Chevy's full size efforts continued, with probably their most famous being the 409-equipped full-size sedans. Immortalized in the Beach Boys song of the same name (yep, that was an engine they were singing about, in case you didn't know!), the 360bhp 409 was

successors) were relatively compact, agile, and they handled comparatively well.

Sporty Chevys

Suddenly the performance bug had bitten America and everyone wanted a piece of the action. Chevrolet, who had arguably been the first to bring performance to the introduced in 1961 and could be ordered on any full size Chevy up until 1965.

Chevrolet were garnering plenty of attention for themselves with the Corvette, America's first successful, home-made two-seater sports car, allegedly inspired by European sportsters which had been flooding onto the market since the Second World War. Launched in 1954, the 'Vette got off to a shaky start, selling in such low numbers that it hardly seemed a commercial viability.

Built using a fiberglass resin body and initially powered by Chevy's wheezy "Blue Streak" straight six engine, it was only once Chevrolet's small block V8 was made available that the Corvette started to set Chevrolet's sales figures alight! The Corvette would go on to be a staple feature in Chevrolet's portfolio of muscle cars, regularly offered with big-block engine options and special performance options.

Right: Another contender for the title of "first muscle car" has to be the Pontiac GTO. Originally an "option" package on Pontiac's mid-size Tempest Le Mans line, it offered really big-block V8 power in a relatively small, agile car.

The Next Step

Ford were working on a similar project to Chevrolet's Corvette, unveiling in 1955 the Ford Thunderbird, an exceptionally handsome-looking car and one which met with far greater commercial success than the Corvette had done initially. The two-seater Thunderbird became a four-seater in 1958 and shrugged off any sporty pretensions it had ever possessed, aiming squarely for the far more lucrative personal luxury sector of the American car market.

Ford's muscle car offering for 1962 was the unassuming-looking Galaxie, fitted with Ford's 385bhp 406cu in V8, which was basically a bored-out version of Ford's FE 390cu in big block, as found in the Thunderbird. Even in 1963, buyers looking for a Ford muscle car were limited to this full-sized combination, as the 425bhp 427 evolved out of the 406 in 1963, and a very handsome fastback-style roofline (called the "SportsRoof") developed on the Galaxie 500XL. Apart from being a great-looking car, it also performed

Above right: Buyers could order cars that were suitable for racing at the drag strip right from the dealership. Cars like this 1964 Thunderbolt could be specially ordered with all the necessary hardware to make an awesome strip machine.

Lower right: Pontiac quickly made a name for themselves in the muscle car era with their Super-Duty Pontiacs. These were specially equipped cars which were designed specifically with drag racing in mind.

awesomely too, winning Ford the 1963 NASCAR title. These cars were also entered for drag strip duty, with fiberglass panels and aluminum components where they met with moderate success. Nevertheless, it seemed as though Ford's "Total Performance" philosophy was now gaining the company a reputation for building winners!

However, by 1964 the tide was turning, and Ford's full-sized muscle cars seemed to be struggling on the drag strip, faced with an onslaught from Chrysler's hugely successful 426 Max Wedges and Hemis. The lighter Dodges and Plymouths underlined something that GM had discovered too, with Pontiac's successful new formula of stuffing big-block engines into mid-size offerings like the Le Mans/GTO. Not to be outdone, Ford took their only mid-size offering, the Fairlane, and shoehorned the 427 engine into it—not an easy task, as the engine bay really would only comfortably accept the 289cu in small-block V8.

Powerful Performers

These Fairlanes, dubbed Thunderbolts, were sent to a Ford contract builder to be modified to accept the oversized engine. Despite the limited production run, they could be ordered from your local friendly Ford dealer for around $4,000. Although technically street-legal, these were really strip cars, and most (103 were built between 1963 and 1965) ended up in the hands of pro drag racers. Every weight saving measure was

Below: Dodge entered the 1960s with some particularly fine drag strip warriors. The 1963 Dodge 330 was a rather dull-looking car, but mated to a 426 Hemi engine it was a real strip screamer.

Above: Chevrolet's full-size offerings were always good-looking cars on the one hand, but when ordered with Chevy's much-admired 409 engine, they were very fast, too.

undertaken with the wholesale use of plexiglass, fiberglass, and no sound insulation. Additionally, a very strip-friendly, but not particularly streetable hand-built version of the 427 came in the package, with solid lifters, twin Holley four-barrel carbs, domed pistons, and a 11.5:1 compression. Buyers could opt for a four-speed T-10 manual 'box or a Lincoln-derived auto.

Ford had set out to win with the Thunderbolts, and boy, did they! The Thunderbolts cleaned up at the S/S Winternationals and the NHRA

Above: The 1961 Chevrolet could be ordered with the engine made famous by the Beachboys' song of the same name: Chevy's 409. It was a 360bhp engine which could take the Impala SS to 60mph in well under 8 seconds and easily achieve sub-16 second quarter-miles. Buyers not so interested in racing quarter-miles could order either a 340bhp or a 350bhp version of the Turbo-Thrust 348 big-block V8.

Above: Chevrolet's Malibu was offered with Chevrolet's performance SS package, but this was mostly cosmetic. For real power, buyers could order a 300bhp 327cu in V8.

Right: Car manufacturers realized the importance of racing. Carroll Shelby worked his magic on the Mustang and today Shelby Mustangs are highly sought after by collectors.

Nationals S/S at Indianapolis and the 1964 Manufacturers Cup, as well as securing the NHRA Top Stock points title.

Over at Chrysler, Plymouth had been doing their bit to bring power to the people since the 1950s with the 1956 Plymouth Fury, a performance optioned sedan that came equipped with a 240bhp 303cu in V8. Rated at 310lb ft of torque, the Fury could hit 60mph in 9 seconds and had a top speed of 114mph. *Road and Track* magazine tested a '56 Fury and were unstinting in their praise of the car's performance: "It has many sports car-like attributes over and above the performance, which is truly 'furious' if not actually sensational."

In only a matter of years, America had come to accept V8 power and horsepower in multiples of hundreds as standard fare—cars were now being judged on their horsepower and acceleration figures alone. The muscle car era had well and truly arrived and, throughout the 1960s, things were only going to get bigger and better!

Accent on the Engine

Chrysler products (Dodge, Plymouth, and Chrysler, generically known as "Mopar" after the parts division which supplies all three) had long been famed for their engineering. It was a well-deserved reputation, as in the early 1960s Chrysler produced some of the most powerful and brilliantly-designed engines ever made. Taking the 410bhp 413 Max Wedge engine

Above: Which was the most respected, legendary, and admired engine of the muscle car era? Probably Chrysler's 426cu in Hemi V8. After its reintroduction in 1960s muscle cars, this car went on to achieve legendary status, and even today "Hemi" cars are widely revered.

(so called due to its wedge-shaped combustion chambers) and shoe-horning it into Dodge's 1962 mid-size Dart resulted in an exceptionally fast package—in fact, by modern standards, a super car. This engine was later bored out in 1963 to 426cu in and was called the Ramcharger. It was available in all Dodges except the Dart, yet it still retained a weight-to-power ratio that made Dodge's Ramchargers almost universally feared at drag strips across America.

Of course, the most famous of Chrysler's engines is the 426cu in Hemi engine, which descended from the aforementioned 413 and 426 wedge RB block. It was so named due to its hemispherical combustion

chambers, an area in which Chrysler had been experimenting since the war, when they had been able to develop exceptionally powerful and fast engines. By 1951 Chrysler actually had their first 180bhp 331cu in Hemi engines available on production cars, and while other manufacturers sold their cars on styling, kudos, and build quality, Chrysler staked their reputation on engineering, as epitomized by the mighty Hemi engine, boring it out over successive years, up to a massive 390bhp 392cu in by 1958. Wonderfully engineered though they were, these engines were not cost-effective to produce, and they were discontinued after 1958.

By 1964 Chrysler had done enough research to enable them to build a bigger block—with a more powerful output, yet without too much extra weight. The 426 Hemi's advantage over the 426 Wedge was that it was able to suck in much more air. As a result

Left: The 1964 Ford Galaxie 500 XL could be optioned with the exciting high performance 425bhp 427 engine.

Above: The 1965 Chrysler 300's interior speaks volumes about what was considered sporty in the Sixties: bucket seats, a console, and four-on-the-floor manual shifter.

Below: The Z/28 option was offered on the 1967 Camaro and featured a 290bhp 302 V8 and Corvette L-69 heads. Designed to handle as well as go fast, the Z/28 was an instant hit.

many sources agree that the advertised 425bhp is a massive underestimate, with the real figure likely to hover around the 570bhp mark! As usual, when it came to drag strip duty, the cars most often chosen were Dodge's mid-size offering, the 330/440/Polara, and the transmission of choice was either Chrysler's rock-solid TorqueFlite auto 'box or four-speed manual. On the strip these cars could regularly achieve 11.4 second/125mph quarter mile times, and rightfully deserved their fearsome reputation.

Nevertheless, it is important to note that fiery and powerful as these engines were, they weren't ideal for street use. So in 1965 Dodge upped the stakes, offering the 426 Street Wedge in its brand-new Coronet intermediate, and in 1966 offered a detuned, street version of the Hemi 426 in the Coronet and the new fastback Charger. Chrysler's motives for reintroducing the Hemi on its passenger cars weren't purely altruistic; they wished to use the engine in NASCAR racing, which meant building at least 500 for sale to the general public.

1960s Styling

At the start of the 1960s, American car buyers were suffering from a hangover from the styling excesses of the previous decade. Suddenly, acres of garish chrome and mile-high fins were no longer popular, as car designers adopted clean-sweep styling with minimal trim and coke-bottle or slab-sided styling. This new ethos of functional design even resulted in

Above: Buick, not normally a division of General Motors associated with muscle car offerings, came up with a very special performance package available on its Intermediate car the Skylark. It was known as the "Gran Sport" package. Buyers got a 325bhp 401 engine, dual exhausts, and a 0-60mph time of 7.8 seconds.

Left: The Sixties were the era of "GT styling." This could mean anything from bucket seats and a console to mag-type wheels, a Hurst shifter or in the case of this Shelby Mustang fastback, a racing stripe right down the middle of the car from bonnet to rear valance.

the launch of the first American compacts, which were introduced to combat the invasion from foreign imports such as the Volkswagen Beetle. These small European vehicles were economical and cheap to run, increasingly proving a popular alternative to American cars, which were generally big and thirsty.

Ford's offering—the Falcon—started off as an austere little six-cylinder car, but went on to become available in a bewildering variety of combinations and bodystyles. Ultimately it provided the basis for Ford's most successful American sports car to date, the Ford Mustang.

Above left: By 1967 the Shelby Mustangs had become the ultimate muscle car. These Mustangs underwent extensive modifications at Shelby's facility and were not only fast, but handled well too.

Above right: Ford may have created a new car market in '64 with the Mustang, but by 1967 Chevrolet had caught up with their pony car, the Camaro.

Introduced in April 1964 at the World Fair in New York, the Mustang took America and the world by storm. The Mustang was a sporty compact available initially only as a two-door notchback or a convertible, but as the years went by the Mustang became Ford's vehicle of choice for showcasing its performance and engineering developments. Probably Ford's greatest publicity coup was the fact that Carroll Shelby chose Ford's Mustang as platform on which to build his new, all-American performance sports cars, the Shelby Mustangs, which remain today probably the most revered outright muscle cars ever built.

While Shelby was taking Mustangs off to his facility near Los Angeles airport and converting them into outright competition machines, Ford were doing a pretty good job of producing their own in-house muscle pony cars. Starting in 1967, when the Mustang was widened and lengthened in order to accommodate the 390cu in big block V8, Ford set about building faster, hairier versions of the Mustang. Over successive years Ford succeeded in this mission, unveiling the mighty 428 Cobra Jet big-block engine and the handsome fastbacked Mach 1 Mustang and the Boss 302, 351, and 429 Mustangs.

Ford had certainly caught General Motors on the hop with the Mustang, as GM had no equivalent (other than the Corvair, which was five years old at the time of the Mustang's launch—and which was considered a bit of an "oddball" anyway). Ford had taken a risk with the Mustang, however

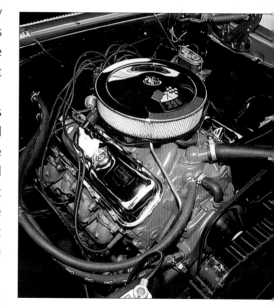

Below: Chevrolet's big-block 396 engine saw service in many Chevrolet muscle cars, from Chevelles to Camaros. Just like the 409, it was the subject of a popular song in the Sixties: *SS396*.

America had taken the sporty little compact to its heart and Ford could barely build 'em fast enough to meet demand.

It took GM two years to reply to the Mustang, but in 1967 Chevrolet unveiled the Camaro, a car based very much on similar principles to the Mustang. A two-door coupe or convertible, it was available with a variety of engines, from an economy-minded 140bhp 230cu in six cylinder, right the way through to 400bhp racing 302cu in Z/28 package. Over at Pontiac, a similar car based on the same floorpan was being showcased—the Firebird—available of course, from mild to wild. The top dog offering in the performance stakes was the Firebird 400, powered by its namesake 325bhp 400cu in V8, available with either a three-speed automatic box, or a four-speed manual.

Ford may have been there first with the pony car, but many felt that Chevrolet and Pontiac hadn't wasted their time in following it up two years later with the Camaro and the Firebird. They were fresh, exciting, and some argued offered much better performance packages than the Mustang. Indeed, it was this stiff competition from GM with their pony car equivalents that spurred Ford onto ever more fiery versions of the Mustang.

Above: As you'd expect, the big Impala boasted all the mod cons. However, bucket seats, a four-on-the-floor, and a tachometer marked it out as special.

More Famous Names

Naturally Chrysler wasn't going to be left out and their initial contribution to the pony car market was the rather tame Barracuda. Introduced on April 1 1964, the Valiant-based fastback failed to disguise its humble underpinning particularly well, emphasizing practicality over performance, with its flat-folding rear seats which offered "7-feet of carpeted 'anything' space." By 1966 the "S" package was offered on the Barracuda, offering a few extra sporting goodies. Equipped with a 235bhp 273cu in V8, the Barracuda was capable of 0-60 in 8.9 seconds and could do the quarter mile in 16.5 seconds, at 84mph. The Barracuda was relaunched in 1967.

Factory-backed racing was important for muscle car manufacturers and the old-adage of "Win on Sunday, sell on Monday" still held true. Plymouth ensured that the Barracuda made a good showing at the 1970 SCCA (Sports Car Club of America) Trans Am series, led by Dan Gurney's All American Racing (AAR) Team. Plymouth was inspired to offer a special 1970 AAR

Above left: The 1968 Ford Torino was available with a variety of engine options, but one of the most popular was Ford's Fiery Cobra Jet V8.

Left: Chevrolet's big-block 427cu in engine saw service in Chevy legends, from the Camaro to the Corvette.

Right: The 1967 Chevrolet Chevelle SS 396 carried all the hallmarks of a real muscle car, from its redline tires to its 325bhp/350bhp 396 V8 engine. Buyers could opt for either a three-speed Turbo Hydramatic or a two-speed Powerglide automatic transmissions.

Left: Chevrolet's Camaro followed the same formula as the Mustang, offering a plethora of engine options—from straight sixes to big-block V8s. There were plenty of appearance options, too.

'Cuda package, offering buyers a 340cu in V8 with triple two-barrel carbs and a very mean-looking appearance package which consisted of rallye wheels, a blacked-out hood, hood pins, and some awesome graphics.

Plymouth had always traditionally been the Chrysler Corporation's cheaper division, just as Chevrolet was for GM. Nevertheless, in 1967 Plymouth saw fit to launch an executive type hot rod, the GTX, which was based on the mid-size Belvedere. It came standard with a deluxe interior and most importantly a Super Commando 440 V8, which was a more powerful (375bhp/480lb ft of torque), yet more driveable version of the standard 440. Buyers also got a TorqueFlite, or an optional four-speed 'box. The only engine option was the street version 425bhp 426 Hemi, making the GTX a real street bruiser. Only 2,500 were built, and of that total 720 were Hemis. GTX sales jumped to 18,940 in 1968, with 15,602 sold in '69.

Above: All the car manufacturers came up with legendary engines during the Sixties: Chrysler had the Hemi, Chevy the 409, and Ford had the Cobra Jet.

New Departures

If the GTX had been Plymouth's interpretation of an "executive" muscle car, then the Road Runner was its version of a "bare bones" entry-level muscle car. Launched in 1968, the Road Runner took the two-door hardtop

Belvedere, and dropped in a modified 383cu in V8 (it featured key components from Plymouth's big block 440). A four-speed manual transmission, and heavy-duty suspension and drum brakes were standard, producing a car which was capable of 335bhp/425lb ft of torque. The only engine option was the Hemi, but buyers could also specify disc brakes up front, limited-slip differentials, and a variety of other performance goodies.

There was a huge market for the Road Runner—in fact, Plymouth had totally miscalculated, expecting to sell only a few thousand in the first year. In reality they sold almost 45,000 Road Runners, and for the following year

Above left: The successful collaboration between Ford and Shelby Industries continued well into the late Sixties. However, later conversions took on more of a cosmetic nature than the serious racing conversions of earlier years.

Above right: Chevrolet's first-generation Camaro was a favorite with specialist dealerships such as Yenko and Dana for big-block, high-performance conversions.

expanded the line-up, offering convertibles and other new and exciting options. What the Road Runner proved was that there was an almost unlimited market for cheap, powerful cars. The late Sixties were a time when insurance premiums were relatively low, gas was cheap, and young people had plenty of disposable income.

General Motors' entry-level divisions, Chevrolet and Pontiac, had long been slugging it out for the crown of performance champion, and in the early '60s it had certainly seemed as though Pontiac was in the lead. Despite pulling out of organized racing in 1963, Pontiac still offered an exhaustive array of engine options. Buyers could choose from the most basic two-barrel 215bhp 389cu in V8, all the way up to a drag strip suited Super Duty 421—available with dual quads and 410bhp and 435lb ft of torque!

The Market Opens Up

The muscle car phenomenon was not limited to the lower end of the car market. Even what were traditionally more upscale car-makers, such as Buick and Oldsmobile, were getting in on the act. However, it was John Z. De Lorean, Divisional CEO of

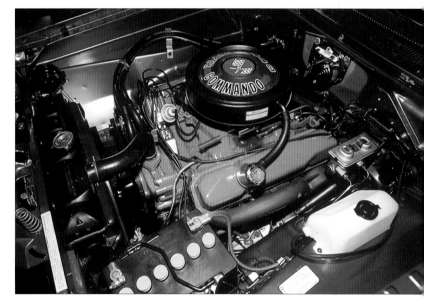

Below: Engines like Dodge's Super Commando were a force to contend with on the drag strip and were serviceable for both racing and daily driving. However, were they thirsty!

Below: Even America's smallest car manufacturer, AMC, got in on the muscle car act. It produced, amongst others, the Rebel Machine, which featured AMC's biggest engine, a 340bhp 390cu in V8.

Pontiac, who well and truly unleashed the muscle car genie from the bottle at General Motors in 1964, by flouting General Motors' self-imposed limit on installing engines no bigger than 330cu in in mid-size cars. Making a special GTO package (a name which had been cheekily borrowed from Ferrari!) available on Pontiac's midsize Le Mans, buyers could take a Plain Jane midsize Pontiac and transform it into a fire-breathing speed machine with only a few strokes of a pen to the options list.

The GTO package consisted of Pontiac's mighty 325bhp 389cu in V8, a four-barrel carb (or optional 348bhp Tri-Power set-up), high-lift cam, and high output heads from Pontiac's high performance 421 engine. As well as a Hurst three-speed shifter, buyers could opt for a Muncie four-speed, and a variety of differentials, including Pontiac's Safe-T-Track limited-slip differential. As one would expect, the package also included a host of heavy-duty extras, from shocks and springs to suspension, as well as a very slick interior with buckets, console, and a fully instrumented dash.

The GTO was an instant success, even with the normally very fussy motoring press, who generally put down American cars in favor of European sports cars. Typical was *Car and Driver,* which was most impressed at test times of 0-60 in 4.6 seconds and quarter-mile time/speeds of 13.1/115mph. Pontiac succeeded in selling 32,450 GTOs in that first year, 8,245 of them equipped with the extraordinarily powerful Tri-Power set-up.

Above: The Dodge Super Bee was part of Dodge's "Scat Pack," a selection of high performance optioned cars in Dodge's line-up. Super Bees could be had with either the 440 or the street Hemi 426 engine. Transmission options included a TorqueFlite automatic or a four-speed manual. Starting prices for the Super Bee were around $3,138.

Left: Equipped with the 426 Hemi, cars like the Super Bee were feared at drag strips across America. However, relatively few were built, so today these cars are sold for top dollar prices. Hemis were available in a number of Dodge and Plymouth cars.

Had the escapade not resulted in unprecedented sales of the powerful Pontiac mid-size cars, the top brass may have been forced to take action against the wilful De Lorean. Instead, each division now demanded their own version of Pontiac's GT/muscle car for the 1965 model year. Chevrolet soon offered the Chevelle SS396, Oldsmobile the 4-4-2, and Buick the Skylark Gran Sport as performance-oriented derivatives of their mid-size compacts. Buick even conjured up a special muscled version of their personal luxury coupe the Riviera, aptly called the Riviera Gran Sport, complete with a host of performance goodies and a 365bhp/465lb ft of torque 425 V8. Dual quad carbs, a limited-slip differential, and 10.25:1 compression ratio meant that Buick's executive cruiser had been transformed into a bona-fide executive express, one which could hold its own at the stoplights and even at the drag strip if so desired. It was a formula which seemed to know no

bounds, as Buick applied their muscle magic across their range, even the full-size Wildcat being offered in Gran Sport derivative form.

By 1966 the GTO had become a series of its own. Since its introduction in 1964, Pontiac had nurtured it and grown it, and for many purists the GTO still represents the essence of what a muscle car is: a mid-size coupe with big block V8 power.

Start of the Slowdown

By the end of the Sixties, muscles cars were a part of the American way of life and were as much a part of America's automotive landscape as station wagons, big

Above centre: Many muscle cars began to develop their own iconography, more often than not based around their engines or the car's name. This is a badge from a Cobra Jet.

Right: The 1970 Shelby GT500 Mustang marked the end of the line for the Shelby Mustangs, which had been offered since 1965. In that time the cars had grown considerably.

Below: Determined not to be left out of the lucrative muscle car market, AMC offered the Hurst SC/Rambler in 1969. It was an unusual-looking car, but definitely a fast one!

luxury sedans and sporty compacts. Yet with this acceptance of muscle cars as a means of mainstream transportation was a growing sense of hostility from a number of sources. Consumer groups were increasingly upset at car-makers' apparent lack of safety concerns. As car manufacturers invested inordinate amounts of money into research and racing programs to make their products faster and more powerful, they appeared to be neglecting safety.

Safety Issues

Automotive safety campaigners such as Ralph Nader openly criticized the big automotive corporations, and indeed a spiraling tally of accidents and fatalities involving these readily available and relatively cheap muscle cars was now starting to attract unwanted attention from both the insurance industry and the Federal Government. Invariably these cars were often pitched at the youth market, and as the insurance industry counted the cost of the devastation that these powerful machines could wreak on the roads in the hands of young and inexperienced drivers, the premiums began to skyrocket.

Left: Sharing much with the Mustang in terms of underpinnings and mechanics, the Cougar was Mercury's upscale pony car offering. Top dog for 1969 was the Eliminator, powered by Ford's legendary Cobra Jet 428 engine. Eliminators came with a rear deck air foil, as seen here.

Right: Taking the "Win on Sunday, sell on Monday" philosophy to its logical conclusion, some car manufacturers began offering virtual replicas of cars competing in races such as the SCCA Trans Am series, like this 1970 Plymouth AAR 'Cuda.

By the Sixties and Seventies another factor was beginning to emerge as an issue which would lead to the eventual downfall of the American muscle car: pollution. As large metropolitan areas such as Los Angeles began to choke on unprecedented levels of air pollution, it became apparent that the Government would have to get involved in controlling vehicle emissions. In California this led to the formation of CARB (the California Air Resources Board) and the involvement of the EPA (Environmental Protection Agency) on a national level.

Above left: Suddenly every car was available with a host of sporty styling options, from hood scoops (which were either functional or not) to air dams and tachometers.

Above right: What your car lacked in pure performance terms could easily be made up for in appearance; Chrysler offered a range of eye-scorching colors during the Sixties.

Soon the Government was dictating what were acceptable levels of emissions and insisting on the introduction of catalytic converters and the detuning of engines. These were all moves which made cars cleaner, but not more powerful.

End of an Era

The final nail in the coffin for Muscle cars was the oil crisis of 1973. This was sparked by the Arab-Israeli conflict the same year and the subsequent oil embargo by the Arab-controlled OPEC oil cartel. Suddenly, America had an acute gas shortage and was looking down the barrel of a gun at the very real prospect of gas rationing. All the while car makers were producing bigger, more powerful gas-guzzling cars, much like the very muscle cars we're celebrating right here. It was time for the Government to step in—this was, after all, a time of national emergency—and as the gas queues stretched around the block and cities faced the prospect of brown-outs, plans were drawn up to downsize America's national fleet.

The Government instructed manufacturers that they were now faced with the prospect of meeting targets in terms of fuel economy and emissions, and it was up to the car-makers to comply or face severe fines on each vehicle produced. And so was born CAFÉ or Corporate Average Fuel Economy. Even fashion seemed to dictate a swing away from muscle

Below: Even manufacturers not traditionally associated with performance vehicles—like Buick—suddenly offered muscle cars, such as the upmarket Buick GSX.

Above: Even small cars got in on the muscle car act, like Plymouth's Duster, which offered a 275bhp 340cu in V8 for some real performance at a low-buck price.

cars, which were evocative of aggressive, macho attitudes, out of synch with the peaceful, loving Seventies, which now embraced eco-friendly, "hippified" vehicles like the Volkswagen camper bus or the psychedelic street van, with murals and shag pile carpeting.

Effectively, a number of different factors combined to make the muscle car extinct by the mid-Seventies. Rising insurance premiums, stricter emission and pollution controls, a rising concern with safety issues, plus the gas crisis of 1973–74—and ultimately even fashion—meant that the demand for muscle cars dwindled and gradually manufacturers stopped putting them out.

Looking at these cars now, it seems impossible to imagine a time when these were just normal cars, available from your local car dealer, but they were, and what wonderful times they were. Welcome back to the muscle car era—enjoy!

Right: Cars like the 1971 Dodge Charger represented the last hurrah of the muscle car era. Gradually they were phased out—victims of government legislation and insurance hikes.

Chrysler

1955 Chrysler
C-300

Above: For many it was Chrysler's 1955 C-300, the car that "swept the field" at Daytona which launched the whole muscle car phenomenon. Designed more in the mold of a grand-touring sports car, it was the epitome of a gentleman's racer, with its handsome "Million Dollar-look" styling, leather seats, and rich interior appointments. Dual exhausts and heavy-duty suspension were standard on the C-300.

Right, and far right: The star attraction of the C-300 was its 300bhp FirePower V8 engine, making it the most powerful car on the market. Dual-quad carburetors meant the C-300 could hit 60mph in a brisk 10.5 seconds, no mean feat when you consider it tipped the scales at 4,340lb! Drum brakes were retained all around, and Chrysler priced the C-300 at $,4109 and sold a total of 1,725 in 1955.

Classic Profile: *1957 CHRYSLER 300*

The 1957 Chrysler summed up all that was great about '50s American cars: exuberant styling, massive tail-fins, lots of chrome, and a big powerful V8 engine throbbing under the hood. The car's designer, Virgil Exner, is to many the "Botticelli" of fins and chrome!

Left: Late '50s Chryslers enjoyed some of the most flamboyant styling of the era, although build quality was often poor.

Right: Chrysler's legendary Hemi Firepower engine could accelerate the 300C to 60mph in about 7.7 seconds flat. Two four-barrel Carter downdraught carburetors help churn out 420lb ft of torque and 375bhp. A 390bhp option was available.

SPECIFICATIONS

Engine	6,424cc/392cu in
Horsepower	375@5,200rpm
Top speed	130mph (210kph)
Wheelbase	219in (556cm)
Weight	4,929lb (2,235kg)
Sales	2,402

Left: Chrysler's 1965 300L epitomized the philosophy behind Chrysler's "Letter Car" concept. It was a handsome, luxury two-door coupe, loaded with style and good looks. It was both glamorous and comfortable, but not only that, it was a real tiger on the road, with phenomenal performance capabilities, which totally belied its appearance. In many ways, Chrysler's 300 series was the ultimate "gentleman's racer."

Below: Many a stoplight racer must've been caught out by the 300L, mistaking it for its humbler (and slower!) New Yorker or Newport, both of which shared the same dimensions and much in the way of sheetmetal as the 300. That little red, white, and blue medallion was a clue to what lay beneath the hood: a 360bhp Firepower 360 engine.

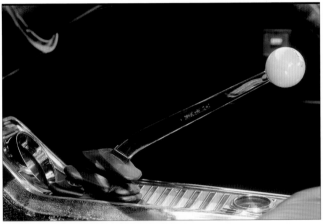

Above: The 300L could be ordered with a no-cost optional four-speed manual transmission if so desired. This was floor-mounted in the console, with a tachometer gauge immediately behind. A vacuum gauge was substituted on TorqueFlite-fitted cars.

Right: The 300L, like all Chrysler products of the mid-Sixties, bore the hallmark of design genius Elwood Engels. Engels gave Chryslers of the period their distinctive long, low look, with sweeping clean sides and "cantilevered" roofs.

Left: The 300L could accelerate from 0-60mph in 8.8 seconds and do the quarter-mile in 17.3 seconds@82mph. The 413cu in was a powerful beast which was rated at 360bhp@4,800rpm and 470lb ft of torque@3,200rpm.

1971 Dodge Challenger

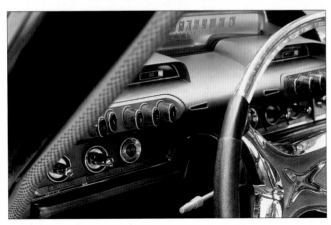

Above and right: While Chrysler had the 300 series, Dodge had the D-500 Ram Induction engine option package. Available on the Dart and the ritzier Phoenix, it consisted of massive cast-aluminum intake manifolds sitting astride a 310bhp 361cu in V8. Despite the Phoenix's massive proportions (almost 17½ft long) and weight (4,120lb), the D-500 Ram Induction engine was able to hit 60mph in almost 8 seconds, with an estimated top speed of around 110/115mph. Not bad performance for such a big, heavy car!

Left: Push-button transmission controls were a popular feature on Chrysler products during the '50s and early '60s. Other glitzy touches included see-through plastic steering wheels and uplit perspex horizontal speedometer.

Right: Despite their quirky love-it-or-hate-it exterior styling, early 1960s Dodges were very conventional inside. Polara 500s were not the most popular choice for racing, compared to other bare-bone models, as they were loaded down with extra trim and equipment which slowed them down on drag strips.

Below and right: The 1962 Polara 500 was the plusher of Dodge's offerings for that year. When fitted with the 413cu in Max Wedge V8 engine it truly was a beast of a car, capable of producing over 400bhp and 470lb ft of torque. Dodge called its version of the 413 the Ramcharger 413, and its wedge-shaped combustion chambers contributed to the engine's distinctive name.

Classic Profile: *1966 DODGE CHARGER*

Fastbacks were big news in the mid-60s and Dodge came up with surely one of the best looking fastbacks ever with the 1966 Dodge Charger, based on the mid-size Dodge Coronet. Although 37,344 Chargers were built in 1966, only 468 were ordered with the legendary 426 Hemi V8 engine. Now that's rare!

SPECIFICATIONS

Engine	426cu in
Horsepower	425bhp@5,000rpm
Top speed	130mph (210kph)
Wheelbase	117in (297cm)
Weight	3,499lb (1,587kg)
Sales	468

Left: The 426 Hemi engine is a Chrysler legend, yet it was relatively rare. Hemi-equipped Chargers could do the quarter mile in around 14 seconds and 0-60 in about 6 seconds.

Below: The Charger boasted a very practical interior, including rear seats which folded completely flat. The dashboard was electro-luminescent giving off an eerie glow at night.

Left: Motoring writers of the time praised the Charger's handsome good looks, including its hide-away headlights and full-width rear lights. It was available with a variety of engines and transmissions, including Chrysler's famed TorqueFlite automatic transmission.

Left: Although a Hemi Charger is probably one of the most sought after muscle cars of the mid-'60s, in reality only relatively few were built. The standard engine was the 318cu in V8, with 361 and 383cu in V8 engines also available. Hemi-equipped Chargers came with all sorts of extra equipment to cope with the extra power that engine produced. This included thicker torsion bars and springs, and bigger brakes. Disc brakes were also available as an option.

Above right, and right: The Charger boasted one of the most stylish interiors of the time, with bucket seats, dash-mounted tachometer, and tasteful use of brushed aluminum trim. A very practical rear load area was achieved by folding the rear seats completely flat. Chargers saw duty in Grand National stock car racing, where they swept the board in 18 races.

Left: The 1967 Dodge Coronet R/T came standard with the 440 Magnum, capable of 375bhp@4,600rpm and 480lb ft of torque@3,200rpm. This particular car is fitted with a four-speed manual transmission. A Hemi engine was available for $907.

Below and right: The Charger was based on the Coronet, so the two cars shared a lot of features, although few would disagree that the Charger was the more handsome of the two. Period features include console-mounted tach, bucket seats, and a full-length console.

Above: Dodge's 1969 Dart Swinger 340 was its entry level muscle car aimed at the budget-end of the market. Priced at a modest $2,836 it came packed with performance goodies, including dual exhausts, a four-speed manual transmission with Hurst shifter, D70x14 wide tread tires, and heavy-duty Rallye suspension. Only 20,000 were built.

Right: A 275bhp four-barrel 340 V8 powered the Dart Swinger 340. Although not as massive or as powerful as some of Dodge's other engines, the Dart's smaller, lighter body meant the car benefited from an excellent power-to-weight ratio. The Dart Swinger also carried Dodge's Scat Pack signature of a bumble stripe over the rear end.

Classic Profile: *1969 DODGE SUPER BEE*

Like its Plymouth Sibling the Roadrunner, Dodge's Super Bee brought affordable performance to the man on the street. The standard Super Bee came equipped with a 335bhp 383 engine, but the 440 Six Pack upped the stakes with multiple carburetion and awesome performance. A bumble bee stripe and scoops topped it off.

SPECIFICATIONS

Engine	7,211cc/440cu in
Horsepower	390@4,700rpm
Top speed	129mph (208kph)
Wheelbase	117in (297cm)
Weight	3,765lb (1,708kg)
Sales	27,800

Above: At the heart of the Super Bee 440 six pack was a 390bhp Magnum 440 engine, topped by a trio of Holley two-barrel carbs. Quarter mile times were around the 14 second mark at 104mph, and 0-60mph was achieved in under 7 seconds. Torque figures were equally impressive at 490lb ft @ 3,600rpm.

Right: Dodge's Super Bee logo summed up the car perfectly—fast and fun!

Above and right: The 1969 Dodge Coronet R/T was Dodge's high performance, high specification offering, with the Magnum 440 engine as standard. "Six Pack" carburetors (three two-barrel Holleys), Ramcharger fresh air induction, and a plethora of axle options made the Coronet R/T a street racer's dream. A Hemi engine could be had for $418. 7,238 Coronet R/Ts were built in 1969.

Left: Twin hood scoops fed fresh cold air into the engine as part of the Ramcharger induction system.

Above and right: The 1969 Dodge Charger Daytona was designed to win back the NASCAR championship from Ford for Dodge, making use of aerodynamics. The massive rear wing and fiberglass nose cone made the car slippery around the track, helping it reach speeds of up to 200mph. However, Dodge had to make at least 500 available for sale to the public in order for the car to legally qualify for stock car competition.

Left: The 375bhp 440 Magnum was the standard offering, although there were a number of Dodge Charger Daytonas equipped with the Hemi engine. Dodge contracted the work to convert the cars to a company called Creative Industries.

Above: Dodge's engineers went to work on the '68 Charger to try and produce a more aerodynamic, faster car for NASCAR racing. Slipstreaming the front grille, and blending in the back window, resulted in the Charger 500, so named in reference to the NASCAR ruling that at least 500 production cars had to be built in order to qualify.

Right: Only 392 Charger 500s were built as a result of a relaxation of the NASCAR rules. Standard power was the 375bhp 440 Magnum, but a number were built with the 425bhp 426 Hemi engine. Transmissions were either TorqueFlite automatic or a four-speed manual box. Quarter mile figures were an impressive 13.6 seconds at 105mph.

Left (both photographs): For 1970 the Dodge Coronet wore fresh, new, sheet metal up front, with a flamboyant new split grille. Side scoops featured R/T call outs.

Above: The 440 Magnum was the standard engine, although the 426 Hemi was available. Once again, TorqueFlite or a four-speed manual transmission were available.

Left: The Dodge Coronet Super Bee came standard with the 383 Magnum V8 and three-speed manual transmission. The Hurst shifter seen here was a smart option. Priced at $3,074, it was actually cheaper than the previous year's model and carried more features, however sales dipped to 15,506 cars.

Above: The Super Bee was one of the cars in Dodge's "Scat Pack," a collection of high performance, fun cars. These cars were collectively marketed to the youth market and were a great sales success.

Right: Dodge Super Bee buyers could choose from a host of psychedelic-inspired color schemes for their cars, including Hemi-Orange, Go-Mango, Plum-Brazy, and Sublime. Likewise, the car's graphics became more wild.

Left: The 440 Magnum was the standard engine, but a small number with Hemis were built. The 440 Charger R/Ts like this one were capable of doing the quarter mile in 15 seconds at 98mph and were good for 375bhp and 480lb ft of torque.

Above: The 1970 Dodge Charger used the same body as the previous year and boasted heavy duty shocks, suspension, and drum brakes, as well as TorqueFlite transmission. Starting at $3,711, 10,337 Charger R/Ts were built that year.

Classic Profile: **1970 DODGE CHALLENGER R/T**

The Challenger was Dodge's offering in the Pony car wars. Like the Mustang or Camaro it was available in a bewildering variety of options and packages, however the R/T package was the one most likely to get performance enthusiasts' pulses racing. A 383 engine was standard, but the 440 Magnum was available as a $250 option. There was even a six-pack option, too.

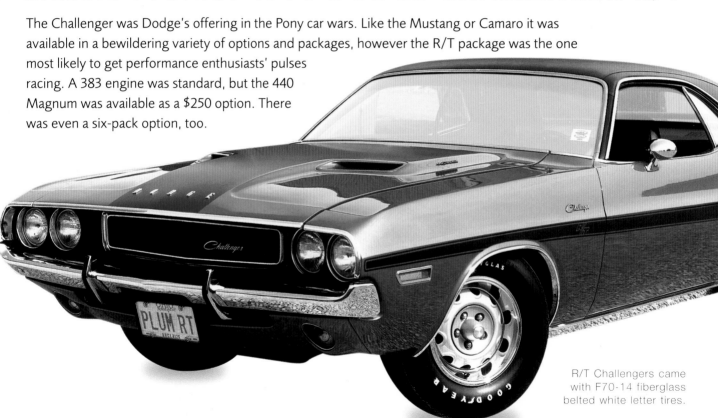

R/T Challengers came with F70-14 fiberglass belted white letter tires.

SPECIFICATIONS

Engine	6,277cc/383cu in
Horsepower	335@5,000rpm
Wheelbase	110in (279.4cm)
Weight	3,402lb (1,543kg)
Sales	19,938

Right: A $250 option on R/T Challengers was the 440 Magnum engine, rated at 350bhp@4,000rpm, and 425lb ft of torque@3,400rpm. A hotter cam option boosted horsepower to 375.

The Challenger R/T was available in three body styles: two-door hardtop, formal hardtop, or convertible.

Left: R/T-equipped Challengers came with a Rallye gauge cluster, and electric clock as standard. Heavy-duty suspension, shocks, and brakes—as well as Bumblebee stripes and special R/T badging—came with the package, too.

Above: The 1970 Challenger T/A was designed with the Sports Car Club of America's (SCCA) Trans Am racing series in mind. It utilized a snorkel-type hoodscoop and side-exiting exhausts, as well as a matt black hood secured with lock-pins. Big E60-15/G60-15 front/rear tires meant the Challenger T/A had to be jacked up in the rear.

Right: Dodge went to work on their 340cu in V8, and used a six-pack carburetion to produce a car which could hit 60mph in only 6 seconds and which could do quarter miles in 14.5 seconds. A total of 2,500 cars had be built in order for Challenger T/A to qualify to compete in Trans Am racing.

Right: T/A goodies included semi-metallic front disc and rear drum brake linings, rear decklid spoiler, a variety of performance axle ratios, and dual exhausts. Color options were as vibrant as ever—this T/A is in Plum Crazy.

Above: By 1971 the muscle car era was drawing to a close. The Charger, however, was restyled that year, and in keeping with the '60s styling of the time the interior was awash with white pleated vinyl and plastic wood. The Charger R/T was priced at $3,777 and came with the usual heavy-duty equipment such as a chrome pedal dress-up kit.

Right: Charger R/Ts came with a 440 Magnum engine as standard, and a very small number were fitted with 426 Hemi engines which was a $707 option. Fitted with twin Carter four-barrel carburetors and with 10.25:1 compression ratio, these Hemi Chargers could produce 425bhp and were feared up and down drag strips across the country.

Left, and far left: This 1971 Plum Crazy Challenger is fitted with a 383cu in V8. It features a Shaker hood, so called as the air scoop, which is attached to the air cleaner and which protrudes through the bonnet, literally shakes with the engine. These particular Challengers have become icons of the best of Mopar muscle, from their curvaceous coke-bottle styling to the awesome power of their mighty, big-block engines.

Above: As a Mustang and Camaro contender, the Challenger was available with a variety of engine options, starting with the smallest 198cu in slant six, going all the way up to the mighty 426cu in Hemi. A total of 29,883 Challengers were built in 1971. Only a few cosmetic changes were made to the car for 1971, which was available in three body styles: coupe, hardtop, and convertible. Prices started at $2,727.

Right: The 1971 Dodge Dart Demon 340 was a sales success, selling over 10,000 cars. However, the name proved controversial, upsetting religious organisations across the United States. The Dart Demon nameplate was replaced from 1973 by Dart Sport.

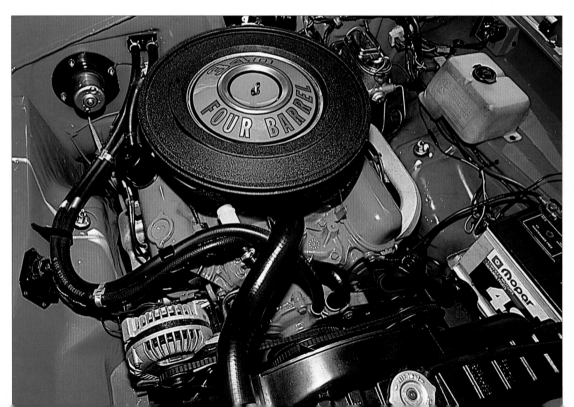

Left: 340cu in and 275bhp made for a very quick package in a relatively small car. Interesting options on the Demon 340 included a deluxe interior, rear spoiler, dual scoop hood with lockpins, and four-speed manual or TorqueFlite transmission. Regular Dodge Darts were positively tame by comparison, utilizing Dodge's 198cu in slant six.

Above: The Dodge Demon was Dodge's compact performance offering for 1971. Buyers got dual exhausts, heavy duty suspension, E70-14 tires, a three-speed manual transmission with floor shifter, Rallye instrumentation, lots of eye-catching decals, and lurid paint. This Panther Pink Demon 340 was definitely not for shy and retiring types!

PLYMOUTH

1967 Plymouth Belvedere GTX

3

Right: 1960 was to be the last year of big fins, and they didn't come any bigger than the 1960 Plymouth Belvedere! Despite its incredible size, the Belvedere was quick off the mark, hitting 60mph in just 9 seconds.

Below: Under the hood sits a massive 330bhp 383cu in V8 part of the SonoRamic option which includes a cross-tube tuned intake manifold, drawing through two four-barrel carburetors. Gas mileage tended to be in the low teens.

Left: Probably the most flamboyant of Chrysler's products for 1960, the Plymouth Belvedere was one of the last designs by stylist Virgil Exner to wear his trademark fins. Design details included push-button transmission, and a square steering wheel.

Above: For 1965 Plymouth offered two versions of its 426cu in big block. The Super Stock Max Wedge rated at 415bhp/425bhp (with 11.0:1/13.5:1 compression respectively) was really a racing engine. The 426-S was the street version, and although officially it was rated at 365bhp, experts reckon the figure was closer to 410bhp.

Right: This 1965 Plymouth Satellite epitomizes for many people what muscle cars are all about: a mid-size car wrapped around a big, powerful engine. Fitted with the street version of Plymouth's 426 Wedge, it utilized a single four-barrel carburetor, 10.3:1 compression, and was capable of 15.2 second quarter miles and 0-60 in under 7 seconds.

Above and right: The 1966 Plymouth Belvedere was one-step down from the plush Satellite, but when equipped with a 426 Hemi, it was a car with few contenders. Standard was the 383cu in V8, but by shoe-horning in a Hemi, buyers could expect blistering performance: 0-60 in 5.3 seconds, quarter mile times of 13.8@104mph, and a top speed of 130mph. Brakes were 11in drums all round, and could be a handful.

Left: Styling on Chrysler's mid-'60s products was clean, crisp, and uncluttered with chrome or trim. A new ethos of "fuselage" styling had taken over in Detroit, as less became more and slab-sided styling took over. Models like the Belvedere put Chrysler in the lead for producing handsomely styled cars.

Right: More upscale than its cousin—the 1966 Plymouth Belvedere—the Satellite carried more trim and equipment. Hardtop roof styling still looks attractive.

Left and below: The street version of the Hemi was a potent powerhouse when combined with the mid-size Satellite. With 425bhp and 490lb ft of torque, it made for blistering performance.

Classic Profile: *1967 PLYMOUTH BARRACUDA*

In 1964, the Ford Motor Company released the Mustang out into the automotive world . A sporty compact, available with a wide variety of options, it created a highly lucrative section in the US car market that had hitherto not existed. And so the "pony car" market was born. Every manufacturer wanted a slice of the action, and for Plymouth, the car they offered was the Barracuda.

Left: In 1967 the Barracuda became its own line, rather than just being a Valiant derivative. The Barracuda came in three body styles: fastback, notchback, and convertible. Prices started at $2,270 for the notchback. Sales were good, totalling 62,534.

SPECIFICATIONS

Engine	6,277cc/383cu in
Horsepower	280bhp
Wheelbase	108in (274cm)
Weight	3,500lb (1,588kg)
Sales	62,534

Right: With 10:1 compression ratio and a Carter four-barrel carb, the 383cu in V8 was rated at 280bhp. It reached 0-60 in around 7.2 seconds. Formula S Barracudas had beefed up suspension and anti-sway bars. Available on the options list were a Sure-Grip differential, front disc brakes, bucket seats, and console.

Left: According to *Motor Trend* in May 1967, the Barracuda suffered from having a fairly limited selection of engine options, and that if buyers did choose the 383 engine, then they could not order power steering or air conditioning.

Above: The 1967 Plymouth Belvedere GTX was Plymouth's first serious attempt at putting together an "off-the-peg" performance package in its mid-size line-up. Like the Pontiac GTO and Oldsmobile 442, the idea was that buyers could order a car with all the performance goodies as a package.

Right, and far right: The GTX hood ornament lets everyone know what's under the hood: a 375bhp Super Commando 440cu in Wedge V8. Dropped into the relatively compact Belvedere body, blistering performance was just a touch of the gas pedal away—0-60 in 7 seconds!

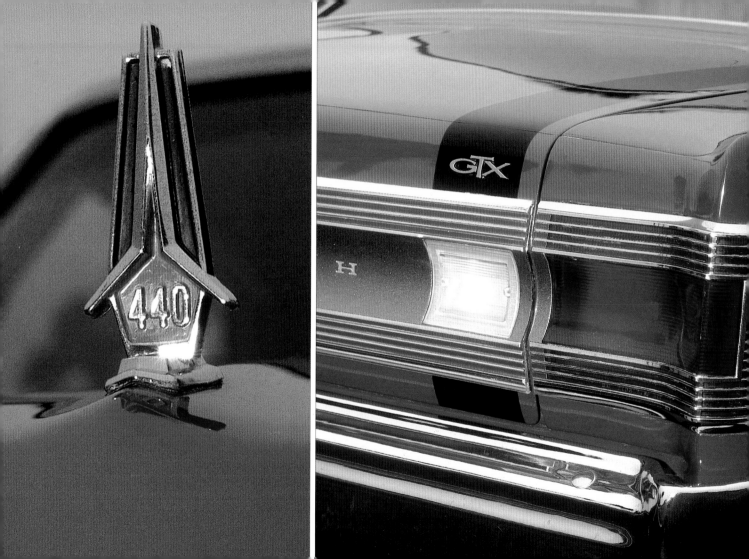

Above: Although the Road Runner may have appeared frugal on the outside, under its hood lay something truly precious. The standard engine was the 335bhp 383cu in V8, but for an extra $714 (almost a quarter of the price of the car itself!), buyers could opt for Plymouth's 425bhp 426 Street Hemi. Roadrunners were available as two-door sedans and hardtops.

Right: Plymouth cleverly exploited the low-buck muscle car market with the 1968 Plymouth Road Runner. Based on the entry-level Belvedere, the car was truly a Plain-Jane special, with rubber mats and a bench seat. Plain dish wheel covers and Red Stripe tires completed the austere look. Aimed at the youth market, Road Runners started at a mere $2,870.

Right: Based on the Belvedere, the GTX offered muscle car buyers more equipment than they could expect to find in a Road Runner. Prices started at $3,329.

Below: Despite offering more goodies, GTX sales were less than half those of the Road Runner, which proved itself to be a runaway success story.

Right: GTXs came standard with the 375bhp Super Commando 440cu in V8. Performance was the name of the game, and 0-60 times of under 7 seconds and quarter-mile times of 14.6@96mph were achievable. For an extra $605, buyers could upgrade to the the 426cu in Street Hemi.

Left: This 1969 Plymouth 'Cuda wears all the trademarks of '60s muscle car styling, from a floor-mounted shifter, to bucket seats, and a console. Federal safety laws required deep dish steering wheels and padding to minimize injury in an accident, hence the awkward, last-minute steering wheel center cap. Under the hood sits a 340cu in V8 engine.

Above: 1969 was to be the last year for this Barracuda shape before it was totally restyled for 1970—it needed it too, as it was definitely starting to look a little old-fashioned when compared to the Mustang, Camaro, and Firebird. Nevertheless, Plymouth persevered, trying to make it look as sporty as possible, with Red Stripe tires and body stripes.

Left: The 383 was the standard Road Runner engine for '69, but buyers could opt for a 440cu in or 426cu in Hemi. Hemi Road Runners could do 0-60 in around 5 seconds.

Above: Chrysler licensed the Road Runner cartoon character from Warner Brothers and even created a horn that went beep-beep!

Right: The Road Runner continued to be a Plymouth sales success story well into 1969. A convertible now joined the line-up.

Right: Base engine for the 1969 Plymouth GTX remained the 375bhp Super Commando 440cu in V8. Equipped with this engine, these cars easily turned in sub-14 second quarter-miles and could hit 60mph in under 6 seconds. The GTX was highly rated by motoring critics.

Above: The bare bones Road Runner still proved more popular than the GTX, which sold in relatively few numbers, totaling just over 19,000 models for 1969. Standard equipment included anti-sway bars, heavy-duty torsion bars and suspension, a 70-amp battery, and F70 x 14 tires.

Left: 1970 was the third and final year for this Road Runner body style. Available as a coupe, two-door hardtop, and a convertible, Plymouth now offered a three-speed manual transmission as standard, rather than a four-speed. Prices started at just below $3,000.

Below: The 383 engine was still the standard offering, but buyers could opt for either the 426cu in Hemi or the 440cu in with six-pack carburetion. Buyers could enjoy a variety of options, including a Super Trak Package designed with racers in mind. This consisted of a heavy-duty manual, four-speed transmission, and a 9 /iin Dana Sure Grip 3.55:1 rear axle.

Classic Profile: *1970 PLYMOUTH SUPER BIRD HEMI*

Chrysler's bid to take back the NASCAR Grand National Championship in 1970 was the Plymouth Road Runner Super Bird. Fitted with a huge wing on the back and a nose cone on the front, the design was aimed at making the Super Bird as aerodynamic as possible. To qualify, NASCAR rules stipulated that at least 500 cars must be built.

Above: Because NASCAR racing had set a 7.0-liter engine limit on cars competing in the NASCAR Grand National competition, the only option for manufacturers was to make their cars faster through the use of slipstreaming and aerodynamics.

SPECIFICATIONS

Engine	6,982cc/426cu in
Horsepower	425@rpm
Top speed	200mph+ (320kph)
Wheelbase	116in (295cm)
Weight	3,935lb (1,785kg)
Sales	135

Left: It's hard to imagine selling what were virtually race cars—capable of over 200mph—to the general public, but to qualify for NASCAR, that's what Plymouth had to do. Less than 2,000 Super Birds were built, and today they remain one of the most highly sought after and highly prized Mopar muscle cars on the market.

Above: The Super Birds were available with two versions of Plymouth's 440 engine (the 375bhp Super Commando and a six-pack 390bhp version), as well as the 425bhp 426 Hemi, which was used in competition. So successful were Chrysler's winged warriors that a Super Bird even won the Daytona 500 that year.

Right: Plymouth had one of the most highly regarded portfolios of performance vehicles in 1970. Dodge may have had the Scat Pack, but Plymouth had its Rapid Transit System, as the range of cars were collectively known. The 1970 Super Bird was just one of these hi-po cars.

Above: How do you spot a Hemi? The plug leads going into the valve covers is always a sure sign. Richard Petty was lured back from Ford to race for Plymouth again after Plymouth began its own aerodynamic program to make its cars faster.

Right: Hemi power came to the Barracuda in 1970 when the car was completely restyled and enlarged slightly to fit the mighty 426cu in lump.

Left and below: Hemi-equipped cars were known as 'Cudas and were a $871 option. Twin four-barrel Carter carbs helped the 'Cuda put out 425bhp. Only around 650 Hemi 'Cudas were built.

Above: Plymouth had its eyes on the Sports Car Club of America (SCCA) Trans-Am racing series when it developed the 1970 Plymouth AAR 'Cuda. In order to qualify for the series, at least 1,900 vehicles fitted with the special racing equipment had to be built and offered for sale. Plymouth built over 2,700 cars, so qualified to race that year, but didn't win.

Right: AAR 'Cudas came with Plymouth's 340cu in engine and lots of racing goodies, including side-exiting exhausts, four-speed manual gearbox with Hurst shifter or TorqueFlite automatic transmission, a special racing bonnet with hood scoop, a spoiler, and plenty of decals, and striping. Production models were available with six-pack carburetion.

Left: The GTX made a final appearance as part of the Belvedere line-up for 1971. It was also the last year Plymouth offered the Street Hemi in any of its cars. This car was considerably bigger-looking than its predecessor.

Above: This Sasafrass Green 1971 GTX is powered by a 440 with three two-barrel carbs. It also has a mean-looking air grabber hood. GTX models were priced at around $3,700.

Right: Engine options for the '71 GTX started with the 375bhp Super Commando 440. The Hemi was still available (just) as a $746 option and an air grabber hood was standard.

Right: Like Dodge's Demon, Plymouth offered a mighty little compact in the shape of the '72 Plymouth Duster 340. Use of special graphics made it fun.

Below and opposite page: Plymouth's entry-level muscle car came with a 340cu in V8, a three-speed manual transmission, dual exhausts, and a wallet-friendly price tag of $2,313.

CLASSIC MARQUES

BUICK

4

1971 Buick GSX Stage I

Classic Profile: *1965 BUICK GRAN SPORT*

Buick has never really been a car manufacturer associated with muscle cars. However, the company did build some very hot performance machines during the 1960s and early 1970s. The '65 Gran Sport, as you can see here, is a classic example.

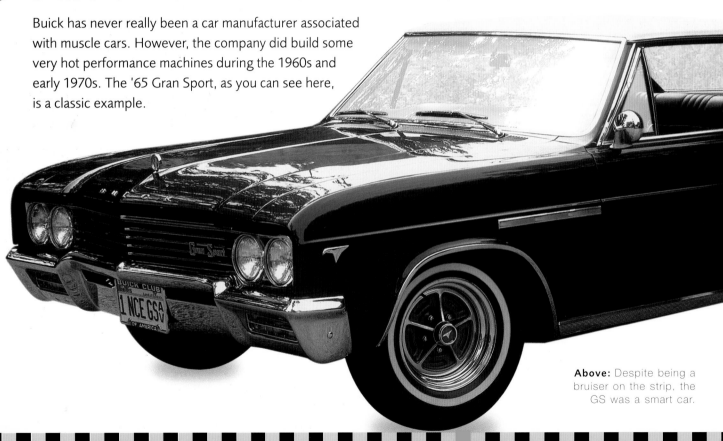

Above: Despite being a bruiser on the strip, the GS was a smart car.

The 1965 Buick Skylark started at $3,149, about $450 more expensive than a regular Skylark.

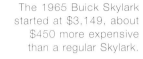

SPECIFICATIONS

Engine	6,600cc/401cu in
Horsepower	325@4,400rpm
Top speed	116mph (187kph)
Wheelbase	115in (292cm)
Weight	3,720lb (1,687kg)

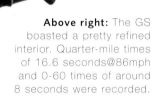

Above right: The GS boasted a pretty refined interior. Quarter-mile times of 16.6 seconds@86mph and 0-60 times of around 8 seconds were recorded.

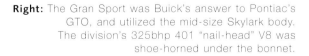

Right: The Gran Sport was Buick's answer to Pontiac's GTO, and utilized the mid-size Skylark body. The division's 325bhp 401 "nail-head" V8 was shoe-horned under the bonnet.

Left: Often dismissed as not really deserving of Buick's proud "Gran Sport" moniker, the GS340 was in many ways a styling package rather than a muscle car like the GS400. The 340cu in V8 engine was the same unit that was available on virtually every other mid-size Buick, and was rated at a lowly 260bhp and 365lb ft of torque. Standard transmission was a four-speed manual, and two-speed Super Turbine automatic transmission was available from the extensive options list. Prices started at $2,850.

Right: Some would say the GS340 was "all show and no go." Certainly it had the looks of a muscle car, with twin hood scoops, sporty stripes, GS badging, and red rallye wheels. The options list even included such performance goodies as heavy duty suspension. Sadly, there just wasn't much under the bonnet. For the real thing, buyers instead would have to order Buick's GS400.

Left: The GSX was a special limited edition model from Buick in 1970. Only around 678 were sold, so these cars are pretty rare. GSXs were only available in Apollo White and Saturn Yellow. Standard was a 315bhp 455cu in engine, however a 345bhp Stage 1 version was also available.

Below and right: GSX buyers got G60-15 Wide-Oval tires, a hood-mounted tach, 3.421Positraction rear axle, front and rear spoilers, a four-speed manual transmission with Hurst shifter, heavy-duty suspension, and power front disc brakes. The GSX carried a hefty price tag at $4,479 and was effectively a $1,199 option package on the GS455.

Left, and far left: Cars like the 1971 GSX were Buick's last gasp in the muscle car era. The GSX package could be ordered with the 260bhp 350cu in V8 standard in Gran Sports, or with the 315bhp 455 as seen here.

Above: Fewer GSXs were ordered in 1971 than in 1970, so are very rare. Government regulations reduced compression ratios in 1971 and subsequently horsepower figures. Stage 1 455 GSXs still produced 345bhp and 460lb ft of torque.

Right: The 1971 Buick Gran Sport was somewhat understated compared to the flamboyant GSX, yet in many ways, this was more in keeping with Buick's "good taste" image. The Gran Sport and GS455 made up almost a quarter of Buick's sales for the 1971 model year. Quite the "Gentleman's muscle car," the GS455 came with all the amenities buyers expected in a Buick.

Left: Despite looking every bit the most civilized of Sunday cruisers, the 1971 Buick Gran Sport was a bit of a handful, especially if the engine had the Stage 1 tuning option. There were 8,268 Buick GS and GS455s built for the '71 model year.

Above: Buick offered its famed 455 engine in the GS, rated at 330bhp in standard form. When tuned up to Stage 1, it put out a total of 345bhp, down on the previous year due to a federally-mandated drop in engine compression ratios.

Above and right: By 1973 the Buick Gran Sport was a mere shadow of its former self. Government and EPA regulations had strangled both performance and styling. Massive federally-mandated impact bumpers and ugly colonnade styling (designed to be safer in a roll-over situation), marred the GS's good looks. Somehow, the 455 Stage 1 managed to struggle on under the hood, but these cars were extremely scarce. This ultra-rare four-speed manual model is believed to be one of only seven built.

Left: Don't forget that Buick GSs were, at the end of the day, still Buicks. Cars like this one still came with everything a Buick customer would expect and want—right down to white vinyl bucket seats and rallye wheels.

CLASSIC MARQUES

CHEVROLET

1972 Chevelle
SS454

Right, and far right: 1961 saw Chevrolet's line of full-size cars totally restyled, including the loss of their fins. Kicking the habit of ever-increasing girth, which had been the trend during the '50s, the new '61s were actually smaller than their predecessors.

Below: For the performance fan, the SS option was the only choice. This '61 Impala was ordered with a Turbo-Thrust 348cu in V8 and four-speed manual.

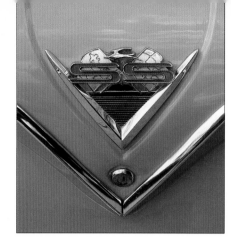

Classic Profile: *1961 CHEVROLET IMPALA SS 409*

Chevy dealers had great news for performance enthusiasts in 1961. The 1961 Chevrolet Impala could be ordered with two engines, including the 348cu in Turbo-Thrust, which came in either 340bhp or 350bhp versions with four-barrel or triple-two barrel carb set-ups respectively. The other engine, which has since gone on to be a legend (it's the one the Beach Boys sang about!), is the 409cu in V8 which was available with three different carburetor set-ups: a four-barrel (360bhp), triple two-barrel (380bhp) or dual quads rated at a whopping 409bhp.

SPECIFICATIONS

Engine	6,703cc/409cu in
Horsepower	360-409bhp
Top speed	150mph (240kph)
Wheelbase	119in (302cm)
Weight	3,555lb (1,612kg)
Sales	142

Right: The Impala featured boasts Chevy's awesomely powerful 409 engine, and was ordered with the SS package, available on all Impala sedans, and hardtops. SS buyers got a four-speed manual transmission, tachometer, heavy-duty shocks and springs, 8x14 white line tires, special wheel covers, and badging. Really the whole muscle car phenomenon had yet to take off, but these were its beginnings: full-size muscle.

Right: Fitted with a 409 the Impala made a formidable bruiser on the strip. The Top Stock Eliminator title was taken in 1961 at the NHRA Winternationals in a '61 Impala with a 409. Dual-quad 409 Impalas are recorded as having made 12.8 second passes up the quarter mile strip. Regular four-barrel 409s clocked 15 seconds.

Below right: Any '61 Impalas fitted with the SS package are relatively rare beasts. It's surprising, really, when you consider the SS package only cost a little over $50. Still, these were the early days of the muscle car era and America was still getting over the styling excesses of the '50s—the need for speed had yet to bite!

Above: This particular car is fitted with Chevrolet's close-ratio four-speed manual transmission. When fitted with Chevy's legendary 409 engine, which in 1962 was rated at 409bhp with a double barrel carburetor, it was capable of quarter mile times around 13 seconds, hitting up to 115mph.

Right: Chevrolet's 1962 Bel Air was one step down from the plusher Impala series, but it was available in the eye-catching two-door hardtop "bubble-top" body style. Bel Airs differed from their more expensive Impala siblings with the use of double taillights, rather than triple taillights, and less trim.

Left, and far left: This car was ordered exclusively for drag strip service and came with all the appropriate options, including a T10 four-speed manual transmission, dual-quad 409, positraction axle with a 4.56:1 rear end. Aluminum panels made it lighter and faster, and were a rare option known as Z11.

Above: Factory specials that competed in Super Stock drag racing are some of the most highly prized cars among collectors. This 1962 Chevrolet Impala SS was delivered to Zintsmaster Chevrolet in Kokomo Indiana and competed widely that year, easily clocking up 12 seconds @ 115mph.

Above: In 1963 Chevrolet offered its 409 engine in three different flavors, the most powerful of which cost only $428 and consisted of a high-lift cam, 11.0:1 compression, dual four-barrel carburetors, dual exhausts, and solid valve lifters, resulting in 425bhp—perfect for a street sleeper like this!

Right: The great thing about the 409 was that it could be ordered in virtually any Chevrolet whatsoever, even a wagon. Hence, the four-door sedan pictured here, which was ordered with a 409 and a four-speed manual transmission, is believed to be very rare indeed, possibly the only one of its kind.

PROFILE

Classic Profile: *1964 CHEVROLET CHEVELLE SS*

1964 was a landmark year for Chevrolet, which offered the mid-size Chevelle (in upscale Malibu trim) with a host of engine options, starting with the 194cu in or 230cu in sixes for the economy-minded. Those more tuned-in to performance would have been attracted by the 250bhp L30 and 300bhp L74 versions of the 327cu in V8. Most intriguing, though, was the 365bhp L76 version borrowed out of the Corvette.

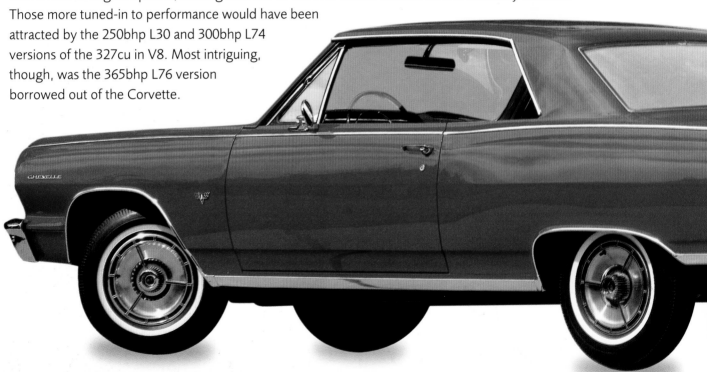

SPECIFICATIONS

Engine	5,359cc/327cu in
Horsepower	300@5,000rpm
Top speed	115mph (185kph)
Wheelbase	115in (292cm)
Weight	2,975lb (1,349kg)
Sales	67,100

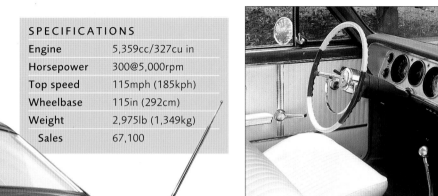

Left: The Super Sport package consisted of a console, bucket seats, and special badging. Order it on a Malibu Chevelle and buyers got themselves a veritable pocket rocket.

Below: In response to the emergence of muscle cars, like the Pontiac GTO and Pontiac F-85, Chevrolet had to offer its customers something. The Chevelle Malibu fitted the bill nicely, having an excellent power-to-weight ratio.

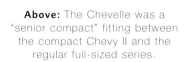

Above: The Chevelle was a "senior compact" fitting between the compact Chevy II and the regular full-sized series.

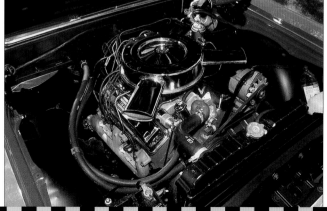

Left: For 1964 the Impala SS became series of its own in Chevrolet's line-up. Available as a hardtop ($2,947) or convertible ($3,196), the Impala SS was still available with three different versions of the Turbo-Fire 409, the most expensive version ($484) rated at an impressive 425bhp.

Above: The Super Sport package consisted of a console, buckets seats, and plenty of badging. Fitted with 409, Impala hardtops could cover the quarter mile in just over 15 seconds and hit 60mph in around 7.5 seconds. Not bad times for a big car which weighed well over 3,500lb!

Left: A select few 1965 Chevelles were built with the very rare Z16 option. These cars not only came with the Chevelle's first big-block option, but were over-engineered in terms of performance goodies, including a convertible frame, 11in brakes all-round, and a Muncie four-speed transmission.

Above: Originally it looked as if the Chevelle wasn't going to get a big-block option, however the limited availability Z16 package offered Chevy buyers a chance to order the new L-37 375bhp 396cu in V8 engine which was destined for service in Chevy's full-size all-new Caprice, and the Corvette.

Above: Cars don't come much more beautiful than the 1965 Impala SS. Chevrolet's styling department really excelled themselves in putting together a car which looked good from every angle, with handsome triple taillights, and wide good-looking grille. Fitted with the 409, the Impala SS was not just practical, and smart looking—it was fast too!

Right, and far right: The 409 came in two versions for '65: a 10.0:1 compression ratio rated at 340bhp, and another 11.0:1 ratio rated at 400bhp. Full-size cars had gained several inches in length and over 100lb in weight, so powerful big blocks like the 409 made sense in such big cars. These 340bhp equipped 409s were capable of sub-17 second quarter miles.

Above: Chevrolet decided to field a Super Sport version of its compact Nova in 1966. Ford had shown there was a market for sporty compacts with the '64 Ford Falcon Sprint, which came with V8 power, bucket seats, console, and a four-on the floor shifter option, now Chevrolet had one of their own!

Right: Fitting the Chevy II Nova with the hot L79 327cu in small-block V8 optional engine (as in the car shown here) made for some amazing performance: 350bhp and 360ft lb of torque. These cars could do the quarter mile in just over 15 seconds and hit 60mph in just over 7 seconds.

Far right: The 1966 Chevrolet Chevelle SS 396 enjoyed a handsomely restyled body. SS styling features included unique wheel covers, and red stripe tires and simulated hood scoops.

Below and right: This particular '66 was fitted with the ultra-rare L78 engine, a 375bhp/415lb ft of torque hi-po engine capable of sub-7 second 0-60 figures.

Classic Profile: *1967 CHEVROLET CAMARO Z28*

Just about every manufacturer went racing during the '60s and Chevrolet was no exception. Their contender in the Sports Car Club of America's Trans-Am series was the Camaro Z/28, which was powered by a 302 small-block V8, due to the SCCA's engine capacity limitation of 305cu in. Although officially listed as putting out 290bhp, many believe the actual figure was closer to 350bhp. Torque was rated at 290lb ft and Z/28s were not only awesomely fast (0-60 in under 6 seconds!) but handled beautifully too, with a top speed of almost 125mph.

Left: The Z/28 option was priced at around $358, but came with a list of other mandatory options which could easily push the Z/28's price well over $4,000. Redline tires and special rallye wheel center caps gave the car a distinctive racing flavor.

Right: Mixing Chevrolet's 327 block, 283 crankshaft, and L79 Corvette heads combined to make a super powerful 302 small block.

Above: The Z/28 has remained one of Chevrolet's proudest performance nameplates, in use until very recently.

SPECIFICATIONS

Engine	4,949cc/302cu in
Horsepower	290bhp@5,800rpm
Top speed	124mph (200kph)
Wheelbase	108in (274cm)
Weight	3,480lb (1,578kg)
Sales	602

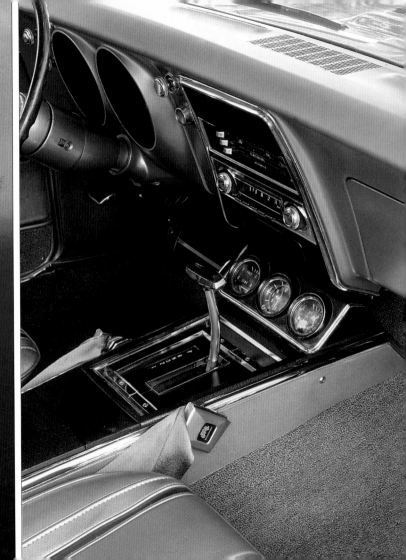

Left, and far left: Chevrolet offered the Rally Sport appearance package in the inaugural year (1967) of its Mustang-beating Camaro. It had been developed to compete in the new burgeoning pony car market and was an instant success. The Camaro SS competed against the Mustang GT.

Above: This 1967 Camaro has the RS appearance package, hence the hide-away lights and blacked-out grille. It also has the performance-inspired SS option, which in this case includes a 396cu in V8 available in either 320bhp or 375bhp versions, both of which were available only in SS Camaros.

Above: The L78 396 engine was one of many available to the Camaro buyer off an extensive options list. The L78 produced an advertized 375bhp and cost around $550 with all the other mandatory SS options that it entailed. A 325bhp version of the 396 engine was also available and cost $235.

Right: Initially Camaro SS buyers were offered Chevrolet's 350 small-block V8, however this was joined later in the model year by two versions of its super powerful 396, available only in SS-equipped cars. Following the Mustang formula, a massive list of options were offered.

Right: Chevrolet launched its Mustang beater, the Camaro, to much applause in 1967. However, for a really hot version of the car, buyers had to approach one of the dealerships specializing in creating "factory hot rod" versions of the car, like Dana Chevrolet of South Gate, California. Dana took Camaros and dropped in a hot big-block 427cu in engine, instantly creating a car that could impress on either the strip or on the street. Buyers also got heavy-duty shocks and clutch, a Muncie four-speed manual, positraction axle, D70x14 Firestone Wide Oval tires, and metallic brake linings.

Left: Dana sold their Camaros for $3,995, no small amount back in '67 (remember a base Camaro listed for $2466). However, for that price buyers got a car vastly faster than any of the factory versions, capable of doing the quarter mile in under 13 seconds @ 110mph.

Left: After its major facelift the previous year, Chevrolet made precious few changes to its 1967 Chevrolet II Nova SS. Buyers got bucket seats, or as Chevy called them, "Strato buckets," special full-wheel covers, a sporty steering wheel, a blacked-out grille, and plenty of badging. This particular car is a rare version, boasting Rally wheels, front disc-brakes, and the powerful L79 350bhp 327 V8, which was deleted in '67, except for a handful of special order installations. Also available was a four-speed manual gear box, metallic brake linings, and tachometer. Bizarrely the Nova SS was even available with a six.

Right: Nova SS hardtops started at $2,467 and sales broke the 10,000 unit mark. These were a drop from the previous year, doubtless due to the introduction of the Camaro, which offered the same compact practicality as a Chevy II Nova in a much more exciting, good-looking package.

Left: The 1967 Chevrolet Chevelle didn't differ dramatically from its '66 predecessor. Red stripe tires, plenty of SS badges, a blacked-out grille, and twin air scoops came as standard. Engine options were limited to either the 325bhp L35 or 350bhp L34. Apparently, the 375bhp L78 option could still be created with parts from your friendly, local Chevy performance parts counter. Automatic transmission options now included Chevrolet's three-speed Turbo HydraMatic, as well as the two-speed Powerglide.

Right: An after-market tachometer keeps an eye on the the mighty 396's revs. Equipment like this is vital for acurately shifting a manual transmission-equipped car like this, and making maximum use of power. Chevrolet sold a healthy 63,000 Chevelle SS Malibus for the 1967 model year.

Left (both photographs): The Impala SS 427 was conceived as an image-building car for the entire Chevrolet full-size line, much in the same way the Chevelle SS396 had boosted sales of all the mid-size Chevelles and Malibus.

Above: It's hard to imagine full-size cars like Cheverolet's '67 Impala SS as muscle cars, but when ordered with the SS package and an 385bhp 427 engine, these cars could hold their own against all comers: 0-60 in around 8.5 seconds!

Left: This 375bhp SS396 was ordered with the very rare L89 396 engine option. Around 300 cars were ordered with this engine, no doubt partly due to its price tag of $896.

Below: L89 SS396s with cold air induction could turn quarter-mile times of around 15 seconds @ 99mph and 0-60 in under 7 seconds.

Right: Little changed on '68 Camaros, federally-mandated side safety lights and ventless side windows were the most noticeable.

Classic Profile: *1968 CHEVROLET YENKO CAMARO*

Don Yenko of Canonsburg Pennsylvania was one of the number of dealers who turned their attention to building big-block versions of the Camaro for sale to performance-minded buyers. Yenko took brand-new Camaros and dropped in Chevy's high performance 427 "Rat" big block. These were offered in either 435 or 450bhp ratings. So popular were Yenko's Camaros that he couldn't keep up with demand for his conversions. Factory-installed 427 Camaros were built instead and ordered using GM's COPO ordering system from 1969.

SPECIFICATIONS

Engine	6,998cc/427cu in
Horsepower	450bhp@5,600rpm
Top speed	140mph (225kph)
Wheelbase	106in (269cm)
Weight	3,145lb (1,426kg)
Sales	64

U·S·A·1
SEE THE USA
CHEVROLET

Right: Inside, there was little to differentiate a Yenko Camaro from a regular Camaro. The magic all took place under the hood.

Above: Yenko and other specialist performance dealers like him proved there was a demand for big-block Camaros.

Right: 427-equipped '67 Yenko Camaros could hit 115mph on the quarter mile and produce 460lb ft of torque. Yenko Camaros were a force to be reckoned with on the drag strip.

Left: SS 396 buyers got a floor-shifting three-speed manual transmission as standard or an optional close-ratio four-speed. F70-14 red stripe tires, simulated air intakes on the bonnet, and plenty of striping and badging all added to the car's racing feel. Well over 57,000 SS 396s were sold in '68.

Below: Chevy's performance fans sighed with relief when the 375bhp version of the 396 was made available again for 1968. The standard engine was still the 325bhp version.

Right: For 1968 the Chevelle line got new sheetmetal, with fastback styling, and an upturned front bumper, and grille treatment. Wheelbase was shortened to 112in, although the car's overall length increased to just over 197in.

Left: Still flying the performance flag for Chevrolet's big cars in 1968 was the Impala SS427. These could be ordered in three body styles: custom coupe, sport coupe, or convertible. Chevy's campaign to woo full-size car buyers with performance failed, and only around 1,800 SS 427s were built.

Above: Costing $358, the L36 427 Turbo Jet V8 produced 460lb ft of torque @ 3,400rpm and 385bhp @ 5,200rpm. On the other hand, opting for the L72 version of the 427 ($542) translated into a very respectable 425bhp and 460lb ft of torque respectively.

Above: The 1969 Camaro Z/28 came with a 302 small block with 11.0:1 compression, solid lifter camshaft, and the ability to produce some staggering times. Quarter-mile times were around 14.3 @ 101mph. The Z/28 package included lots of other performance equipment and cost around $450.

Right: From its introduction in 1967, the popularity of the Camaro Z/28 grew each year, and by 1969 the sales figures had jumped to a remarkable 20,302 units. Key to the car's popularity was its high profile in the Sports Car Club of America (SCCA) Trans-Am racing series.

Right: COPO Camaros, such as this 1969 model pictured here, were cars ordered through Chevrolet's "Central Office Production Order" system (hence COPO). It was the only way the Camaro could be ordered with Chevrolet's big-block 427 engine from the factory. The alternative was relying on a specialist dealership, like Yenko or Dana, to install one afterwards.

Right: Complete with "poverty" wheel trims (the most basic, entry-level hubcaps), the implication is that all the money that's been spent on this car went under the hood! Prices for COPO Camaros started at around $3,500.

Right: 427-equipped Camaros were much favored among drag racers of the late-'60s, so it's no surprise that a thriving business grew installing 427s. Dealerships across America became famous for upgrading cars and tweaking them so they would clean up at the drag strip. Dealers like Dana Chevrolet, South Gate, California and Don Yenko, of Cannonsburg, Pennsylvania became legends—and their cars even more so.

Classic Profile: **1969 CHEVROLET CAMARO ZL1**

The 1969 Camaro ZL1 represented one of Chevrolet's biggest commitments to performance and racing. In response to pleas for a ZL1 aluminum 427-equipped Camaro from Chevrolet dealer Fred Gibb, Chevrolet built 69 cars with the ZL1 to qualify in NHRA Super Stock (which stipulated that at least 50 cars must be built). Fifty cars were shipped to Gibbs' dealership, with the other 19 sent elsewhere. ZL1-equipped cars came with dual-exhausts, power brakes and steering, racing mirrors, and F70-15 plain Jane blackwall tires. The original price was $4,900 per car, however this rose to over $7,000!

SPECIFICATIONS

Engine	6,965cc/425cu in
Horsepower	430bhp@5,200rpm
Top speed	130mph (210kph)
Wheelbase	108in (274cm)
Weight	3,135lb (1,422kg)
Sales	69

Above: A ZL1 Camaro might look pretty plain, but like all the best sleepers, it's what the exterior doesn't tell you that says everything!

Right: The ZL1 Camaros meant business on the drag strip, recording quarter-mile passes of 10.4 seconds at over 128mph. A ZL1 Camaro campaigned for Gibbs' dealership is recorded as having achieved a 10.05 @ 139mph!

The exceptionally low production figures of the ZL1 ensure its high-value collector status today.

Right: Inside the ZL1 Camaro was much like any other—it was only when you stepped on the gas that you found out that this was in fact a Camaro unlike any other! The RS package gave it sporty looks.

Left: Dropping Chevrolet's mighty 427 big-block V8s into the Camaro was undertaken by a handful of specialist performance dealers, such as Don Yenko of Canonsburg, Pennsylvania. By 1969, however, it had become possible to order 427-equipped Camaros via the COPO ordering system.

Above: Don Yenko was one of a handful of dealers who decided to target performance enthusiasts. Others included Fred Gibbs Chevrolet of La Harpe, Illinois, Dana of Southgate, California, and Nickey Chevrolet of Chicago. These factory-built "hot rods" are the Holy Grail to many Chevrolet fans.

Left: The Chevy II name was dropped in 1968, and the car benefited from handsome new styling introduced the year before. The 396 engine was available in two flavors: 350bhp @ 5,200rpm and the more powerful 375bhp @ 5,600rpm. Buyers could also choose from a variety of transmissions, including the standard three-speed manual, a Mucie four-speed (with floor shifter), or a two-speed Powerglide or three-speed Turbo HydraMatic. Chevrolet sold a total of 17,654 SS-equipped Novas, a massive jump from the previous year's sales.

Right: The Nova shared much with the Camaro, including front suspension, front subframe, and floorpan. Indeed many of the engines that fitted the Camaro would fit the Nova. Chevrolet didn't offer the big block 427 in the Nova, so several drag racers built their own!

Left: The 1969 Chevelle SS 396 offered buyers a 325bhp 396, F70x14 white letter tires, a twin power dome hood, dual exhaust, lots of bright moldings, and SS badging galore. Engine options included the L34 350bhp 396.

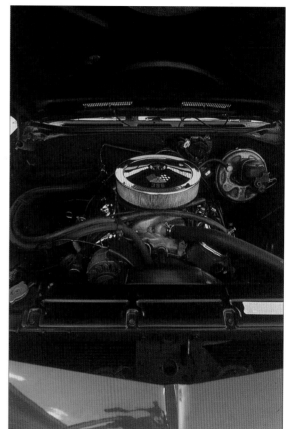

Above: Total cost of the SS package was around $440 and over 86,000 Chevelles left the factory in 1969 with the SS option. Many car fans today agree that the '69 Chevelle SS396 is a muscle car icon.

Right: This L78-equipped SS396 produced 375bhp and could cover the quarter mile in 15.4 seconds—0-60 times were around 7 seconds. A few, very rare COPO-ordered 427 engines went out in Chevelles.

Left: Chevrolet offered a number of engine options on its Chevelle SS line, including 325, 350, and 375bhp versions of the 396 and the very rare 427 engine, seen here. For '69 the SS 396 was changed from being a separate series to an option pack.

Left: Chevrolet's big-block 427 engine wasn't available through regular ordering channels, but had to be ordered through COPO.

Below: This rare SS427 is fitted with Chevy's console with "shopping basket" shifter, and high-back bucket seats.

Left, and right: It's believed that only around 350 Chevelle SS427 cars were built in 1969. Just about all of them are understood to have been shipped to specialist Chevrolet performance dealer Don Yenko in Cannonsburg, Pennsylvania, who had made a name for himself in race circles. This handsome '69 Chevelle SS427 is one such car, and carries unique Yenko hood decals, and head rests. Aftermarket Torq Thrusts give the car a handsome imposing profile. Although Yenko became famous for his 427 Camaros, his dealership worked its drag strip magic on a variety of other Chevy products, including the Nova SS, the Chevelle SS, and even the humble Corvair!

Right: 1969 was the final year for the big 427-powered Impala SS. After three years it had become clear that the market just wasn't receptive to a full-size muscle car. Most full-size car buyers tended to be older and not as interested in performance, rather they were concerned about comfort. The buyers who were interested in performance tended to be younger, and were more interested in mid-size and compact cars like the Chevelle and Nova, which had traditionally been marketed to that particular age group. Subsequently, only 2,455 Impala SS 427s found buyers.

Left: The SS427 was a $422 option and could be ordered on the Impala sport coupe ($3,033), custom coupe ($3,085), or the convertible ($3,261), as seen here. Buyers got 15in wheels with red stripe tires, heavy-duty suspension and chassis, power disc-brakes, and special badging.

Left: The Camaro was totally restyled for 1970, with a new longer, wider look, fastback roof styling, and a more prominent grille. The Z/28 package now cost around $572, and was still popular with buyers, who ordered 8,733 Z/28 Camaros in 1970.

Above: Under the hood the old 302 was replaced with a LT-1 350, with a four-bolt main, solid lifters, aluminum valve covers, and 11.0:1 compression all resulting in a highly impressive 360bhp. The Z/28 could happily do quarter miles in 14.2 seconds @ 100mph.

Classic Profile: *1970 CHEVROLET EL CAMINO SS 454*

Chevrolet didn't limit their muscle car talents to passenger cars ... oh no, they even worked their magic on the car-based pick-up, the Chevrolet El Camino, shoe-horning the big block 454 engine under the hood to produce a lightning fast ... truck!

Above: The El Camino was based on the Chevelle/Malibu, sharing much in the way of trim, underpinnings, and mechanical hardware. The trucks were lighter than the cars.

Pick-ups lead hard lives and few survive, making SS454 El Caminos ultra-rare, as well as ultra-fast.

The El Camino SS came with many of the same goodies found on its Chevelle/Malibu SS counterpart, including a power-bulge hood, four-speed manual transmission, and was an option costing under $400.

SPECIFICATIONS

Engine	7,441cc/454cu in
Horsepower	360bhp@5,400rpm
Wheelbase	116in (295cm)

Right: Big block versions of the El Camino were no strangers to drag strips, easily doing the quarter mile in under 15 seconds @ around 98mph.

Right: The El Camino SS454 surely must be considered the ultimate muscle truck.

Left: For Chevrolet fans the 1970 Chevelle SS 454 represents probably the ultimate in Chevy muscle. By 1970 just about every other manufacturer had upped the stakes in the cubic inches wars, so Chevrolet decided to raise the stakes by offering the Chevelle with a big-block 454 engine.

Above: The 454 came in two versions: the LS5 rated at 360bhp and 500lb ft of torque, or the LS6, rated at 450bhp and 500lb ft of torque. Around 3,773 SS 454s were built for the 1970 model year.

Right: Cars fitted with the 450bhp LS6 could do the quarter mile in 13.8 seconds @ 97.5mph and 0-60mph in 6 seconds. Direct competitors included the 429 Ford Torino, and the 440 Plymouth Road Runner.

Above: By 1970 it was apparent to GM that the big car muscle market was not going to take off. Big car buyers were more concerned with comfort than speed, however, the 454 was offered in the Caprice.

Left and right: Although not boasting the SS assignation which had graced Impalas from '67-'69, the Caprice was still a force to be reckoned with when equipped with the big-block 454. At almost 4,000lb, it was no lightweight, but could still hit 60mph in under 10 seconds.

Above: 1971 was not the best of years for muscle car lovers; federal emission legislation meant lower compressions and less horsepower from engines. Cars like this 1971 Chevrolet Chevelle SS suffered a drop in horsepower. Around 80,000 Chevelles with the SS package were built in '71.

Right: The Chevelle was available in a variety of different guises. The SS package cost $357 and came with a specially domed hood, blacked-out grille, front disc brakes, F60x14 white letter tires, and lots of SS badges. The 454 engine was still available … just.

Left: The 1972 Chevelle was only slightly different from its 1971 predecessor, with a few changes to the grille and turn signal lenses. The SS package was available on any V8-equipped Malibu, from the base 130bhp 307, right the way up to the 270bhp 454, which would make one final appearance the following year, before being dropped in 1974. SS buyers got a special hood with locking pins, front disc-brakes, special gray 15in (F60-15) wheels, sports suspension, and SS badging, all for $350. This car is fitted with the big-block 402 engine. Roughly 25,000 Chevelle SS were sold in 1972.

Right: Sky-high insurance costs for target muscle car buyers in their 20s or younger meant the cars like the big-block SS Chevelles were losing popularity. Chevrolet's answer was to offer appearance packages rather than actual performance-enhancing equipment.

Left: The 1972 Chevelle SS 454 is a rare beast: only 5,333 were built. A four-speed manual transmission was standard, or buyers could opt for Turbo-Hydramatic automatic.

Below: The LS5 engine was rated at 270bhp @ 4,000rpm and 390lb ft of torque, and cost $272 over and above the cost of the SS equipment package.

Left: The 1972 Chevrolet SS 454 represented one of the last hurrahs for Chevrolet's muscle car legacy; the 454 engine would only be offered for one more year, before facing extinction in 1974.

OLDSMOBILE

6

1971 Oldsmobile 4-4-2

Classic Profile: *1965 OLDSMOBILE 4-4-2*

When Pontiac launched the GTO performance option package on their mid-size Le Mans/Tempest line, they succeeded in creating a substantial market for sporty mid-sized coupes and convertibles virtually overnight. Other divisions within General Motors scrambled for a piece of this lucrative segment of new car sales. Oldsmobile's answer was the 4-4-2 which was launched midway through 1964 and was a performance option package available on the Olds' mid-size F-85. For 1965, buyers got a 345bhp 400cu in V8 with a four-barrel carburetor, four-speed manual transmission, and a dual-exhaust, hence the 4-4-2 moniker. The motoring press at the time praised the 4-4-2 for its handling ability.

SPECIFICATIONS

Engine	6,556cc/400cu in
Horsepower	345@4,800rpm
Top speed	118mph (190kph)
Wheelbase	115in (292cm)
Weight	3,735lb (1,694kg)
Sales	25,000

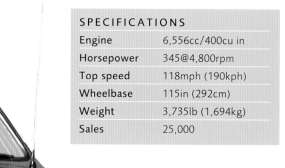

Above: Dummy side air-scoops, wire basket wheels, and redline tires all spelt GT performance in the mid-'60s. The 4-4-2 was a handsome-looking car with manners, as well as brawn.

Right: A 400cu in V8 was able to take the 4-4-2 to 60mph in under 8 seconds and could cover the quarter mile in 15.5 seconds @ 84mph. Transmission options included Jetaway automatic or 3- or 4-speed manual.

Left: For 1966 the 4-4-2 was available with the W-30 package, Oldsmobile's drag race special. Buyers got cold air induction, fiberglass inner fenders, trunk-mounted battery, an engine chrome dress-up kit, and some pretty remarkable track times with it.

Above: A Rochester Quadrajet four-barrel carburetor meant the 400cu in V8 was capable of 350bhp in 1966, however a tri-carb set-up was also available, boosting performance to 360bhp.

Right: Transmission choices consisted of either a 3-speed manual, a 4-speed Muncie manual, or a Turbo Hydramatic automatic. Only 54 W-30 packages were sold in 1966, out of a total of 24,747 4-4-2s sold that year.

Left: The W-30 package remained very much the same for 1967 as in 1966. Cold air was ducted to the engine from the front, and a 3.90:1 Posi-Traction and tachometer meant the W-30 equipped 4-4-2s tore up the tarmac.

Above: Like Buick's Gran Sport option on the Skylark, Oldsmobile's 4-4-2 was more than just a bare-knuckle fighter like some of the other performance machines from other manufacturers; it was a comfortable, civilized car too!

Above: The '69 Hurst Olds utilized the division's big 455 engine which developed 380bhp and 500lb ft of torque. The Hurst Olds could do quarter miles in under 14 seconds at over 100mph, and could hit 60mph in under 6 seconds. Hurst began to get a reputation for helping produce limited-edition super cars like the Hurst Olds.

Right: 1968 saw a total restyle for the Cutlass, with handsome new lines and an exclusive Hurst option which offered Oldsmobile's mighty 455cu in engine under the hood. This option was continued in 1969, finding just over 900 buyers. These were strictly limited production vehicles and are very rare today.

Right: All 1970 Oldsmobile Rallye 350s came with a Force Air fiberglass hood and Rallye Sport suspension. Both 3 and 4-speed manuals were available with Hurst shifters, or a 3-speed auto.

Below: In 1970 Oldsmobile launched the Rallye 350, a kind of bargain bruiser much like the Pontiac GTO Judge. It had eye-catching qualities like bright yellow paint and decals.

Right: Power for the Rallye 350 came from a 310bhp 350cu in V8. However, this could be upgraded with the W-31 forced induction system which boosted horsepower to 325bhp. A typical 310bhp Rallye 350 with a 3-speed manual could do quarter miles in around 15.5 seconds @ sub-90mph speeds and 0-60 in under 8 seconds. Around 3,547 Rallye 350s were built for 1970.

Classic Profile: *1970 OLDSMOBILE 4-4-2 W-30*

The 1970 Oldsmobile 4-4-2 probably epitomizes all that was good about "Dr Oldsmobile," as the ad men had taken to calling the division. 1970 was the first year Oldsmobile was able to overcome the corporate ban on using engines over 400cu in in mid-size cars, and the 455 was shoe-horned in. The W-30 package offered extra performance equipment like the fibreglass hood and transmission options. Dr Oldsmobile had done it again!

Above: As well as being an immensely powerful car, the 4-4-2 developed a reputation as being a car which could handle itself.

Above: The W-30 option was offered on 455 4-4-2s. A similar W31 package was offered on the Cutlass S.

SPECIFICATIONS

Engine	7,457cc/455cu in
Horsepower	370@5,400rpm
Top speed	115mph (185kph)
Wheelbase	112in (284cm)
Weight	3,777lb (1,713kg)
Sales	19,330

Above: Oldsmobile's 455 engine had been unavailable to use in the 4-4-2 before 1970 due to GM's ban on using engines over 400cu in in mid-size cars. This had been gotten around by getting Hurst to install the engines and selling them as special limited-edition cars. The 4-4-2s with the W30 option could easily run quarter-mile times in 14 seconds, often hitting 100mph. The W-30 package also added power front-discs, a fiberglass hood with twin scoops, and a variety of transmission options.

Right: For 1970 Oldsmobile introduced its opulent Cutlass SX, a top of the line model with highway cruising in mind. Simulated walnut appeared opulent.

Left: G70-14 Firestone belted tires made from polyester and fiberglass were designed to give less rolling resistance than conventional tires, and hence improve gas mileage.

Left: Oldsmobile gave the Cutlass SX the full luxury treatment, while ensuring it gave excellent fuel economy, and comfortable highway cruising. This was achieved through a very specific combination of a two-barrel carburetor on the 455 and a 2.56:1 rear axle, all designed to give excellent turnpike manners and relatively low fuel consumption. This meant the SX was no demon off the stoplights, however it could still return respectable quarter-mile times in the 15 second range. Top speed was estimated to be around 117mph.

Right: 1971 was the last year that the 4-4-2 appeared as a separate model. Buyers got the 455 big block, G70-14 tires, stabilizer bars, reinforced springs, and dual exhausts. The W-31 package was dropped from the Cutlass range, however the W-30 package was still available. Due to the drop in compression ratios, the power output of 4-4-2s was dropped down to around 340bhp. Only around 1,304 convertibles were built for the 1971 model year, and around 6,285 hardtops.

Left: This particular car was ordered with the W-27 rearend—an aluminum axle housing which shaved around 20lb of the car's weight. Rallye-style wheels, a hood with air scoops, and special badging marked out the 4-4-2 as a special car.

Above: New colonnade styling was the big story on Oldsmobile's Cutlass for 1973 (as well as all the other GM division's two-door hardtops). The 4-4-2 was now more an appearance package on regular Cutlasses than a separate line of cars. Oldsmobile were particularly successful with the Cutlass throughout the early '70s, and as a division sold 938,970 cars that year.

Right, and far right: The Hurst-Olds combination had become a performance institution, however, by the early-'70s it was becoming more of an appearance package than a serious performance option. Sports console and swivelling sports bucket seats were standard. The Hurst package cost $635. Powered by Oldsmobile's mighty 455, the '73 Olds could boast a 0-60mph time of 6.5 seconds.

Classic Profile: **1974 OLDSMOBILE HURST**

By 1974 the muscle car era had truly drawn to a close. Nevertheless, Oldsmobile made one last splash with the 1974 Hurst Olds. One was chosen to pace the Indy 500 and Oldsmobile manufactured a handful of special "replicas" to celebrate. Buyers could order the smaller 350 Olds engine if they wished, but the 455 was the standard offering.

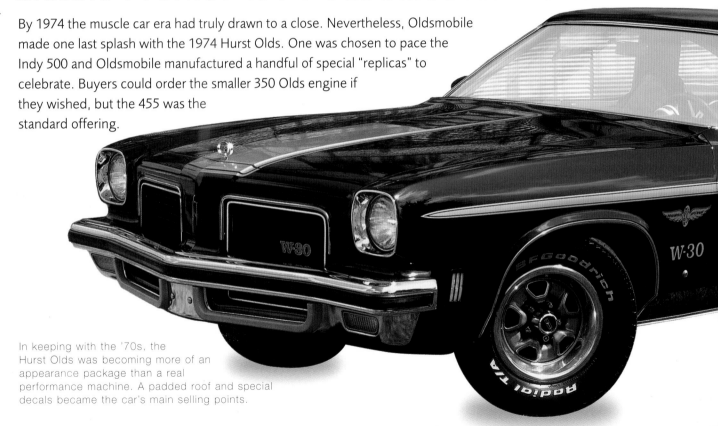

In keeping with the '70s, the Hurst Olds was becoming more of an appearance package than a real performance machine. A padded roof and special decals became the car's main selling points.

SPECIFICATIONS

Engine	7,457cc/455cu in
Horsepower	230@4,000rpm
Top speed	120mph (193kph)
Wheelbase	112in (284cm)
Weight	4,085lb (1,853kg)
Sales	1,200

Top, and right: Under the Hurst-Olds' hood sat Oldsmobile's venerable 455 engine, rated at a meagre 230bhp for 1974. Nevertheless, Hurst still claimed 0-60 times of around 6.5 seconds. The Cutlass was a strong seller throughout the '70s for Oldsmobile.

PONTIAC

1964 Pontiac Catalina 2+2

Left: Pontiac had a mission to clean up at the nation's drag strips in 1962. This it set about doing with its Super Duty Catalinas, like this two-door hardtop. Special aluminum body panels made the cars lighter, hence faster up the strip.

Above: Under the hood a 405bhp 421cu in V8 capable of turning in some extraordinary quarter mile results. It was not unknown for Super Duty Catalinas to be able to achieve 12.4 second times at 116mph! Production was limited to 162 cars.

Left: This 1962 Pontiac Grand Prix is one of only 16 Super Duty Grand Prixs built that year. The 421 engine breathed through twin Carter four-barrel carburetors.

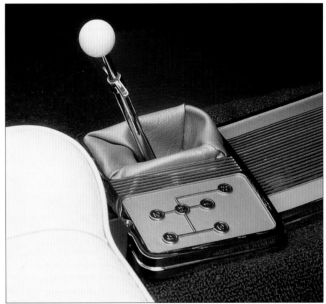

Above: This car is fitted with a four-speed manual transmission. Super Duty engines could put out in excess of 400bhp!

Right: Pontiac's Grand Prix was the top of the line sporty car in '62—the GTO was still a sparkle in Jim Wangers' eyes!

Left: The Pontiac Grand Prix was handsomely restyled in 1963. It was a car which brought glamor and performance to the division. Unique eight lug aluminum wheels, as seen on this car, are a highly desirable and collectible option. The Tri Power 389 engine is rated at 313bhp @ 4,600rpm.

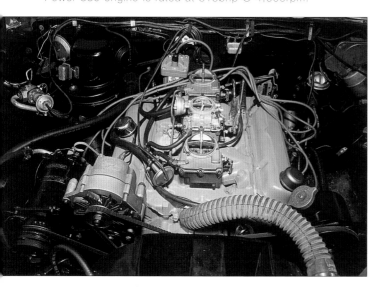

Above: This Grand Prix features the standard 389cu in engine fitted with the optional Tri Power carburetion (i.e. three two-barrel carburetors.)

Right: The Grand Prix boasted a smart interior, with bucket seats, console, and Morrokide upholstery, as well as a wood-grained dash and steering wheel.

Classic Profile: *1964 PONTIAC GTO*

The GTO option was an option package first offered on Pontiac's mid-size Le Mans/Tempest line of cars in 1964. It was an inspired piece of marketing genius, as performance cars were becoming more and more popular with younger buyers. In the GTO package they found all the most popular options brought together in one comprehensive, hot package – it was a hit!

Below: GTOs were relatively light cars at the time, and with their big, powerful 389s, could hit 60 in around 14 seconds.

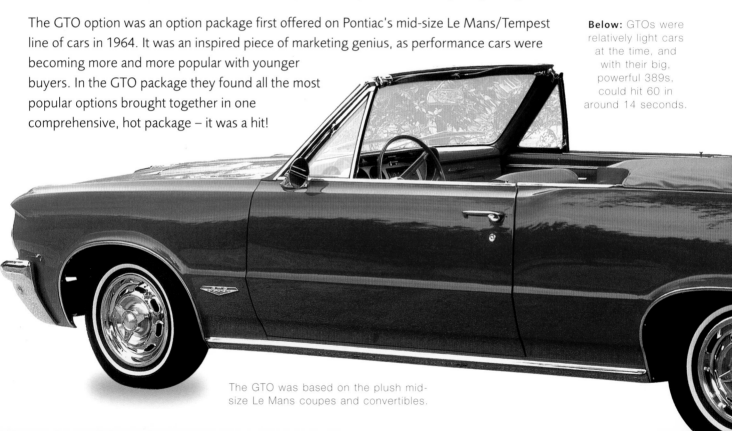

The GTO was based on the plush mid-size Le Mans coupes and convertibles.

SPECIFICATIONS

Engine	6,375cc/389cu in
Horsepower	348@4,900rpm
Top speed	105mph (169kph)
Wheelbase	115in (292cm)
Weight	3,360lb (1,524kg)
Sales	32,450

Right: A sporty interior gave the GTO a really sporty flavor. Bucket seats, four-on-the-floor, and a tachometer, plus a name borrowed from one of Italy's most legendary sports cars translated into a huge sales success.

Lower right: Mixing big-block power with a mid-size coupe or convertible made for a formidable street machine. Pontiac's big 389 engine was rated at 348bhp with Tri Power.

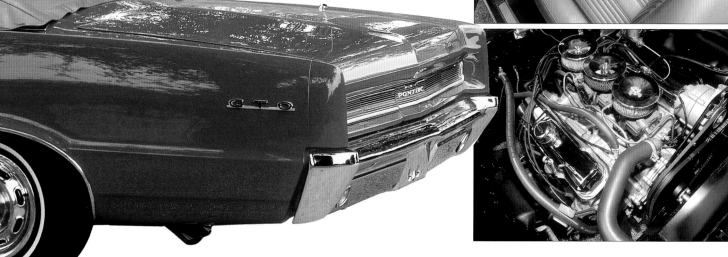

Right: The 2+2 was the first performance package available on a full-size Pontiac along the lines of the GTO option. It was released on the 1964 Catalinas.

Below: The optional 421 came in three different strengths, including a 370bhp Tri Power option. This sporty package wasn't quite as spectacular in the big Pontiacs as it had been in the smaller GTO.

Left: The 2+2 performance option was only available on the big Catalina Sport Coupes and Convertibles. Buyers got bucket seats, a console, and a choice of a four-speed manual or Hydra Matic automatic transmission. Fitted with the 370bhp 421 engine, 2+2s could do 0-60 in just over 7 seconds.

Left: Tri Power remains a popular option on GTOs today. However, 1966 was to be the last year for Tri Power set-ups following a GM ban on multiple carburetion set-ups on all but the Corvette. Tri Power 389s were rated at 360bhp.

Above: 1965 had seen a major restyle on the Le Mans/GTO and in 1966 the GTO became a series of its own, available in three body styles: a two-door hardtop, two-door coupe, and a convertible. These '66 GTOs could do 0-60 in 7.5 seconds.

Left: Ford created a new car segment overnight with the Ford Mustang in 1964. It took GM a couple of years to catch up, with their offerings the Chevrolet Camaro and Pontiac Firebird, but when they did they caused a sensation. Like the Mustang, Firebirds were available with hundreds of options.

Above: Firebirds were available in either two-door coupe or convertible bodystyles and were available in several "model option packages," including the 400 series seen here. The Firebird 400 came with a 325bhp 400cu in engine and three-speed manual, a twin air scooped hood, and upgraded suspension. A hood-mounted tachometer like the one above was a smart detail. The Firebird 400 listed at $2,777.

Right: The '67 GTO carried over many of its looks from the previous year. New under the hood though was a 33bhp 400cu in V8. Tri Power was gone, but a four-barrel and Ram Air could be had.

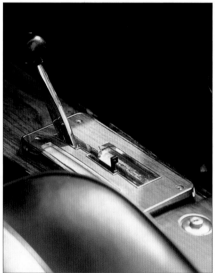

Above and left: Buyers could opt for the "His 'n' Hers" shifter, which allowed the driver to either shift between gears or just leave the selector in "D" and let the transmission do the work.

Classic Profile: **1967 PONTIAC GRAND PRIX**

The Grand Prix underwent something of a transformation for 1967. The craze for hide-away headlights meant they were hidden behind the grille, while turn signals were hidden in recesses in the front wing. Built on a massive 121in wheelbase, the Grand Prix was over 215in in length (almost 18ft). Weighing over 4,000lb, the Grand Prix typified the general trend among American car makers towards building bigger, heavier cars. Cars like the Grand Prix needed bigger, more powerful engines to compensate for all the extra weight and accessories they now carried. Almost 43,000 Grand Prixs found buyers in 1967.

SPECIFICATIONS

Engine	6,556cc/400cu in
Horsepower	290@4,600rpm
Top speed	110mph (177kph)
Wheelbase	121in (307cm)
Weight	4,005lb (1,816kg)
Sales	42,981

Right: The Grand Prix was a big stylish cruiser which carried many classic '60s styling cues, from hide-away headlights to fender skirts.

Right: Sporty styling cues included front strato bucket seats and console. A Grand Prix could be as well optioned as a Cadillac.

Right: The '67 Grand Prix came standard with a 350bhp 400cu in V8. With 4,000lb to haul, the GP was never going to be really fast.

Left: Pontiac's Firebird saw few changes for the '68 model year. Federal safety side-marker lights made use of Pontiac's logo, and vent windows were lost as on the Camaro. Also new was astro-ventilation and suspension upgrades.

Below: The Firebird was available with seven different engine options, ranging from a base 175bhp six, to a fire-breathing Ram Air II 400cu in V8 rated at 340bhp and 430lb ft of torque.

Right: Sales were up on the previous year's figure of 82,560, with 107,112 Firebirds finding buyers. The pony market was crowded now, but it seemed buyers just couldn't get enough!

Above: Engine options for the '68 GTO consisted of four variations on the 400cu in V8 from the previous year. The Standard four-barrel Rochester Carburetor engine was rated at 350bhp and 445lb ft of torque. Next up was a 360bhp/445lb ft of torque version with a hotter cam. But topping the list was a 360bhp Ram Air 400.

Right: For 1968, Pontiac's GTO adopted new coke-bottle styling, with a semi-fastback, flowing flanks, and a unique one-piece polyurethane "endura" bumper which was meant to pop-back into shape if bumped. Hide-away headlights and hood-mounted tach and air scoops all added up to what was quite definitely the "in" car back in '68.

Classic Profile: *1969 PONTIAC GTO JUDGE*

In 1969 Pontiac released a special options package called "The Judge," named after a popular routine off a comedy show of the time. The Judge GTO was meant to offer a lower-priced version of the GTO disguised with plenty of graphics and funky colours. Buyers got a deck-mounted rear spoiler, a front air dam, blacked-out grille, mag-type wheels, a Hurst shifter, and eye-popping psychedelic decals. What really interested car fans was what hardware came with the package: a 366bhp 400cu in V8 Ram Air III engine and a 3.55:1 rear axle, perfect for taking up the strip. Some cars also got the 370bhp Ram Air IV engine. These cars were capable of 14-second quarter miles.

Right: The Judge may not have been the finest handling muscle car, but in a straight line it was hard to beat. Cars like the Judge could be raced the day after they were bought.

SPECIFICATIONS

Engine	6,556cc/400cu in
Horsepower	366@5,100rpm
Top speed	124mph (200kph)
Wheelbase	112in (284cm)
Weight	3,513lb (1,593kg)
Sales	6,833

Right: The Judge was designed to be an economy supercar—but that didn't mean that it had to be spartan. Buyers got a choice of bucket or notchback seats, and a deluxe steering wheel.

Below right: Ram Air 400 engine could be had in 366 and 370bhp versions and would easily take the car to 60mph in around 6.2 seconds.

Left: For 1969 the Firebird got a new front end treatment, with a new-look grille and headlight treatment. Pontiac also took the Firebird racing in the SCCA Trans Am series, resulting in a new model to the Firebird line-up: the Trans Am. Buyers could choose from eight engines, including a 345bhp Ram Air IV.

Above: Despite a restyle and the fact that buyers could now choose from several model options, sales for the new-look Firebird fell to 87,011 units.

Right: The 1969 Pontiac Formula 400's engine was now rated at 330bhp and was available with a Ram Air 400 package costing $350-$430 over the base price.

Above: Pontiac Firebird buyers were confronted by a bewildering array of engine options in 1969. Base engine was still the 175bhp 250cu in six-cylinder, with engines ranging all the way up from two 350cu in V8s to three different 400cu in V8s, including the 345bhp Ram Air IV. Pontiac was ranked as the number three automaker for 1969.

Right: Standard on 1969 Pontiac Firebirds were E70-14 tires, vinyl bucket seats, carpeting, and outside mirrors. The 400s got dual exhausts, heavy battery, chrome engine dress-up kit, and F70-14 redline or white stripe tires. A special hood with non functional scoops (unless Ram Air package was ordered) came as part of the 400 package, too.

Left: Pontiac launched the Trans Am package in 1969, costing $725. A 335bhp Ram Air III engine was standard, with a 345bhp Ram Air IV engine as an option. Buyers also got a limited slip differential and 3-speed manual transmission.

Above: The Trans Am, despite its name, never raced in the race series of the same name. Nevertheless, with 0-60 times of 6.5 seconds and quarter-mile times of 14.3@101mph, there was no doubting their performance qualifications.

Above: The beginning of the '70s were difficult times for muscle car manufacturers. Cars like the GTO faced a shrinking market, and a barrage of government safety and environmental legislation. Nevertheless, Pontiac persevered with cars like the GTO. The Judge option, costing under $400, was a bargain by any standards. Reduced compression meant engines now rated from 300bhp (400) to 335bhp (455).

Right, and far right: "Judge" buyers got all the performance goodies that came with a GTO, but moved up to the 455 HO engine with a T-shifter, and manual transmission, a hood with functional air scoops, rear deck lid spoiler, Rally II wheels, and of course plenty of decals, and outrageous paint. Hardtop Judge GTOs sold for under $4,000. Only 374 Judge convertibles and hardtops found buyers for 1971.

Right: The 1972 Pontiac GTO was virtually identical to the 1971 model. Horsepower rating on the most powerful 455 engines dropped by 350bhp to 300bhp, and sales further slid to 5,807 units. The base engine was a 250bhp 455 which generated 325lb ft of torque. Rather than enjoying the status of being a separate line, the GTO now reverted to being an option package on the Le Mans line once again. The "Judge" option package was dropped for '72, too.

Left: The 1972 Pontiac GTO listed at $2,968 for the hardtop and with the advent of lower compression engines, the GTO wasn't as fast as it had been. Quarter-mile times of 15.5 seconds and 0-60 times of over 7 seconds proved the point.

Left: Pontiac's Firebird had been totally restyled in 1970, adopting a "bull nose" front grille and a more streamlined, fastback profile, appearing longer, lower, and wider. The Trans Am series returned and, for the 1972 model year as seen here, featured a 300bhp 455cu in V8 as standard.

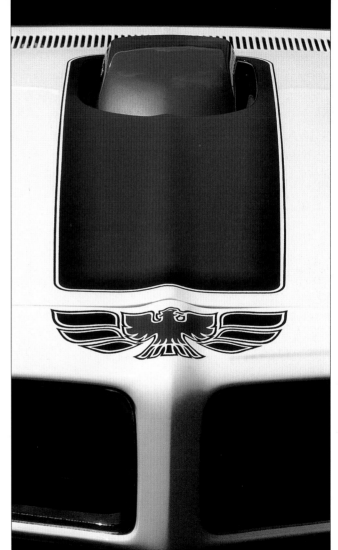

Above: A machine-turned dash and rallye gauge cluster were standard, as was a close-ratio, four-speed manual transmission with floor/console-mounted shifter.

Right: Rear-facing cold air induction system and plenty of decals made the Trans Am stand out. Appearance was becoming more important than performance.

Classic Profile: *1974 PONTIAC TRANS AM*

By 1974 the muscle car era had truly drawn to an end. However cars like the '74 Pontiac Trans Am bravely continued to fly the performance flag for the American car industry. The US auto industry had been thrown into chaos with the onset of a serious gas crisis after the Arab oil embargo, and cars with big engines (or "gas guzzlers" as they were known) were virtually impossible to sell as car buyers switched to more economical cars with small engines, which, more often than not, were imports. The '74 Trans Am was extensively restyled from the previous year, losing the aggressive "bull nose" front end and gaining a much smoother grille. The rise of "appearance" packages over actual performance criteria seemed relentless: the shaker hood was merely cosmetic, as was the screaming chicken on the hood.

Above right: Special Trans Am hardware included a limited slip differential, dual exhausts, rear spoiler, four-speed manual transmission, and F60-15 tires.

SPECIFICATIONS

Engine	6,228/455cu in
Horsepower	290@4,000rpm
Top speed	132mph (212kph)
Wheelbase	108in (274cm)
Weight	3,655lb (1,657kg)
Sales	10,255

Right: Standard in the Trans Am for '74 was a 225bhp 400, with either a 215bhp 455 or the mighty 290bhp SD 455 (Super Duty) engine.

Right: Trans Am buyers got a turned aluminum dash, rallye gauges with tachometer, and a Formula steering wheel. Base Firebirds listed at $2,895, while Trans Ams started at $4,204. The Super Duty 455 engine marked a returning interest in performance at Pontiac, with respectable quarter-mile times back in the 13s @ 103mph.

FORD

1970 Ford Mustang Mach 1

Left: For 1962 Ford unveiled a new 405bhp Thunderbird Special 406cu in engine, which was available in the full-size upscale Ford Galaxie 500XL. Triple two-barrel carburetion, and a four-speed manual transmission made the 500XL fast.

Above: Just another big '60s cruiser right? Wrong! The '62 Galaxie 500XL could turn in 15-second quarter-mile times and reach 60mph in around 7 seconds—not bad for a car which weighed over 3800lb. Galaxie 500XLs began at $3,106.

Classic Profile: *1964 1/2 FORD MUSTANG*

It was the car which launched a whole new segment of the car industry: the Ford Mustang. Even today this legendary nameplate is one of the best known, most well-loved of the 20th (and 21st!) century. The brainchild of Lee Iaccoca, the Mustang was a new type of car: a sporty compact. It was based on Ford's unremarkable little Falcon, but boasted exciting styling and a host of available options.

Left: Mustangs were available in three body styles: notchback, convertible, and fastback.

Above: Introduced at the World Fair in New York on April 17 1964, the Mustang was an instant success, selling 680,989 units for the 1965 model year.

SPECIFICATIONS

Engine	4,736cc/289cu in
Horsepower	271@6,000rpm
Top speed	120mph (193kph)
Wheelbase	108in (274cm)
Weight	2,583lb (1,171kg)
Sales	7,273

Right: This particular Mustang was ordered with the 271bhp HiPo version of the 289. These engines were available from June 1964 and were available only with a four-speed manual transmission.

Right: Ford's "Total Performance" philosophy of selling more cars through racing resulted in cars like this 1964 Galaxie 500, fitted with the 425bhp "R" code Thunderbird Super High-Performance engine. Ford had to offer these engines in regular production cars in order to qualify to race them in NASCAR and on drag strips.

Left: Despite their large size, '64 Galaxie 500s could pound up the quarter-mile strip in under 15 seconds and hit 60mph in 6 seconds.

Above: The 427cu in came with two large Holley carburetors and an 11.5:1 compression ratio. Output was 425bhp @ 6,000rpm.

Above: Ford had high hopes for its full-sized factory race specials. However, these hopes weren't realized, so Ford turned its attention to the mid-size Fairlane, producing the drag race special Fairlane Thunderbolts for 1964.

Right: The ultra-light Thunderbolts came with a 427 officially rated at 42bhp, although experts reckon they were closer to 500bhp. Quarter-mile times of 11.6 @ 124mph meant they did well in NHRA competition and only 111 were built.

Left: To celebrate the anniversary of its introduction, Ford launched the GT option pack on April 17 1965 for the Mustang. This option gave the Mustang a sporty flavor.

Below: The GT package consisted of dual fog lamps, dual exhausts, front disc-brakes, Special Handling package, quick ratio steering, and lots of GT badging.

Left: Fitted with the high-performance 271bhp version of the 289cu in engine, the Mustang could do 0-60mph in 8.3 seconds and the quarter-mile in 15.6 seconds at 85mph. Its top speed was 120mph.

Classic Profile: *1965 FORD SHELBY GT350*

Ford knew the way to boost sales of any car was through racing, and what better way than to get legendary American racer and racing car builder Carroll Shelby involved. Ford shipped Mustangs to the Shelby facility near Los Angeles Airport where the Shelby magic was worked on them, transforming them into high performance machines. These modifications involved everything from improving suspension and handling, to upgrading the standard 271bhp HiPo 289s.

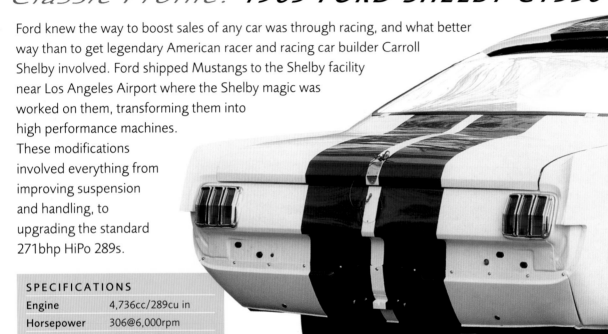

SPECIFICATIONS

Engine	4,736cc/289cu in
Horsepower	306@6,000rpm
Top speed	125mph (201kph)
Wheelbase	108in (274cm)
Weight	2,800lb (1,270kg)
Sales	561

Right: This "R" Code 1965 Shelby Mustang was built specifically with racing in mind. The engine was further tuned to produce 350bhp and the cars came with a roll bar, interior safety group, and an exhaustive array of instruments.

Lower right: Battery was rear mounted and "R" versions also got a 34-gallon gas tank, quick-fill gas filler, plastic windows (which saved weight), and larger radiator and oil cooler.

Above: Large diameter exhausts exited in front of rear wheels. The 15x7 magnesium wheels were also part of the "R" Shelby package.

Right: The Mustang was little changed for 1966—why change a winning formula? This notchback was ordered with the GT equipment group ($152), which was available only on Mustangs ordered with the 225bhp or 271bhp 289cu in V8. Ford sold a total of 607,568 Mustangs for the '66 model year and had little competition from other manufacturers.

Left: Fourteen-inch styled steel wheels like this were only available on V8 equipped cars and were a $93 option.

Above: The 271bhp K-code HiPo 289 engine was the most powerful and cost $276 when ordered with the GT equipment.

Left: Ford updated the 1966 dash on the Mustang, getting rid of the Falcon-derived one which had been used on '65 Mustangs. A deluxe steering wheel was a $32 option.

Opposite page, right: Only 5,469 cars were ordered with the 271bhp 289 engine, which could now be had with the Ford's Cruise-O-Matic automatic transmission. GT equipped Mustangs like this one remain highly collectible today.

Above: Mustangs ordered with the 271bhp "K" code HiPo Challenger V8 could hit 60mph in under 8 seconds and return quarter-mile times of around 16 seconds. Fitted with the Special Handling package, GT Mustangs handled well.

Right: This 1966 Mustang convertible was not ordered with the GT package, however it was ordered with the 271bhp HiPo 289 engine. A real performance engine, this compact little V8 had solid lifters, 10.5:1 compression, and a four-barrel carburetor.

Above: Over 72,000 convertible Mustangs were sold in '66. Plymouth's Barracuda was no competition and the Camaro wasn't ready—Ford had the pony car market all to itself!

Left : The standard engine on Mustangs was a 200cu in straight-six, however buyers could choose from three strengths of 289, from 200bhp to 271bhp.

Classic Profile: *1966 FORD SHELBY GT 350H*

Racing had become so popular during the '60s that not only was it possible for the ordinary man on the street to go out and buy an off-the-shelf racer like the Shelby Mustang, it was soon possible for him to just rent one for the weekend. The enlightened car rental car company which decided to get in on the act was Hertz, which, in 1966, ordered 936 Shelby Mustangs. Most cars were painted black, but some were painted white. The cars were popular to rent for weekend racing, and at $17 a day were a bargain.

SPECIFICATIONS

Engine	4,736cc/289cu in
Horsepower	306@6,000rpm
Top speed	125mph (201kph)
Wheelbase	108in (274cm)
Weight	2,800lb (1,270kg)
Sales	936

Below left: The GT350H (The "H" stood for Hertz) was a great promotional vehicle for Shelby and Hertz. They were, however, only available to rent to members of Hertz's Sports Car Club.

Right: GT350Hs were available with either a four-speed Borg Warner manual or Ford's C4 automatic transmission.

Below right: The breathed-on 289s put out in excess of 300bhp and GT350Hs came with heavy-duty sintered metallic brakes, and upgraded suspension.

Right: Ford's all-out performance war resulted in the big 427 being offered in the mid-size Fairlane in '66. It was available in either 410 or 425bhp ratings, the latter returning 13 second quarter-mile times @ 114mph.

Left and below: The Fairlane was totally redesigned for 1966, including the engine bay to allow for Ford's big-hitting 427cu in big block. Only around 60 such cars were built, but they were great image-builders for Ford.

Left: Ford had the sporty compact market all sewn up in 1966 with the Mustang. However, in an attempt to cater to the full-size performance fan, Ford developed the "7-liter," a sporty version of the Galaxie 500XL.

Above: Most 1966 Ford Galaxie 500 XL 7-liters came with Ford's 428cu in engine. However, a handful—like this car— were built with the race-bred 427cu in engine. Convertibles weighed over 4,000lb and started at $3,844.

Above: The '67 Fairlane differed little from the '66 other than a few minor trim differences. The 427-equipped cars also came with heavy-duty suspension, four-speed manual transmission, 8.15x15 tires. Fitted with the 427 (or the 428), the Fairlane was Ford's answer to the mid-size performance competition, namely Chevrolet's Chevelle SS396 and the Dodge Coronet. Car buyers listened, and the Fairlane was a great seller.

Right, and far right: The 427 big block made a return to the options list for Fairlane buyers and was available in either a 410bhp four-barrel carbureted version, as seen here, or a 425 dual-quad set-up. A big scoop on the fiberglass hood ensured the engines breathed properly. These high performance versions of the Fairlane saw competition on NASCAR tracks, and up and down drag strips across the US.

Left: The 1967 Ford Galaxie 7-liter offered luxurious motoring with a distinctly sporty flavor—this was performance driving GT style. Bucket seats, a console shifter, and deep-pile carpeting lent the cabin an opulent air.

Above: The '67 were restyled, growing an extra 4in in length. Four engine options were available: 345bhp and 360bhp 428cu in V8s, or 410bhp and 425bhp versions of the 427. Weighing close to 3,500lb, the 7-liter was a heavy car.

Left: It's probably the most famous car in cinema—a Highland Green Mustang fastback, similar to the one from the Steve McQueen film *Bullitt* (however, that was a '68 fastback). The Mustang was extensively restyled for 1967.

Above: For 1967 the Mustang grew in length and width, making the engine bay wider to accommodate the Mustang's first big-block option: the 320bhp 390cu in V8, as seen here. Around 28,800 390-equipped Mustangs were built in total.

Above: Probably the most desirable 1967 factory Mustang is the GTA convertible. These were the C4 automatic transmission-equipped cars. They came with F70x14 tires, power front discs, fog-lamps, dual exhausts, and handling pack.

Right: In 1967, 24,079 GT Mustangs were sold. Ford sold 44,808 convertibles, 356,271 notchbacks, and 71,042 fastback Mustangs in 1967. Integral air conditioning rather than hang-on, under-dash units were offered for the first time.

Classic Profile: *1967 FORD MUSTANG GT*

The first generation of Mustang ('65-'66) had offered fastback styling, but it was only in '67 that Ford finally got it right with a handsome new integrated look that truly was a proper fastback. Although the 108in wheelbase remained, everything else grew. Mixed with the GT option package, it was a winning formula.

Below: Fastbacks had rear seats which folded completely flat, offering practical cargo space.

SPECIFICATIONS	
Engine	6,392cc/390cu in
Horsepower	320@4,600rpm
Top speed	125mph (201kph)
Wheelbase	108in (274cm)
Weight	3,262lb (1,479kg)
Sales	24,079 ('67 GTs)

Left: Despite competition from Chevrolet's Camaro, the Mustang was still the original Pony car, and Ford sold 472,121 Mustangs for the 1967 model year.

Above: The GT package cost $205 in 1967. The 390-equipped Mustangs could do 0-60 in around 7 seconds and the quarter-mile in 15.3 seconds @ 93mph.

Left, and far left: The '67 Shelby GT350 utilized a Cobra hi-rise manifold with a 715cfm Holley Carburetor on a 306bhp 289. Total weight was 2,800lb. The 15in Shelby steel wheels were shod with E70-15 Speedway low-profile nylon tires. The 11.3in disc brakes were standard up front.

Above: A special fiber-glass hood, central driving lights, and a unique rear-end treatment, including different taillights from regular production Mustangs, and a spoiler completed the package. Some 1,175 GT350s were built for 1967, and 2,048 GT500s, bringing total Shelby production to 3,223 cars. GT350s listed for $3,995.

Above: Fitted with the rare 425bhp 427cu in V8, developed for NASCAR racing, the 1967 Shelby GT500 was an awesome performer. However, most GT500s got the 355bhp 428, capable of 15.5 quarter miles, 0-60mph in 7.2 seconds, and a top speed of 132mph.

Right: At $4,195, '67 GT500 buyers not only got a car that performed very differently from regular production Mustangs, but one that looked different too. Remember, the largest, most powerful engine available to Mustang buyers in '67 was the 320bhp 390.

Right: The Torino came in three body styles for '68, by far the most handsome was the fastback, called a "SportsRoof." These were available with a GT option package, as seen here, and could be ordered with the 428 Cobra Jet engine.

Above, and left: Two versions of Ford's 428cu in Cobra Jet were available: the 335bhp Cobra Jet, and the 360bhp Super Cobra Jet. The Torino GT package included special badging and wheel center caps.

Left: With the launch of Chevrolet's Camaro in 1967, the Mustang came under pressure, particularly its high performance versions, which were limited to the 320bhp 390 or 271bhp HiPo 289 engines. So for 1968, Ford offered the 335bhp Cobra Jet 428.

Left: Mustang changed little for 1968—a few trim and grille alterations, and federal safety side-marker lights. However, there was a whole roster of new engines on the options sheet, including 302, 428, and 427cu in V8s.

Above: The new-for-'68 Cobra Jet produced 335bhp @ 5,400rpm and 440lb ft of torque @ 3,400rpm. Fastbacks like this weighed 3,240lb and could do the quarter mile in 13.5, and 60mph in under 6 seconds.

Left: The 1969 Ford Mustang was extensively restyled, growing in every dimension except for height and wheelbase, which remained 108in. A more aggressive front end, and higher rear-end and different taillights marked out the '69s, as did ten engine options.

Left: The Cobra Jet 428 was rated at 335bhp and was a $287 option. Hardtop Mustangs started at $2,618. 1969 was the last year that bench seats were available in the Mustang, and was the first year for a four headlight set-up.

Above: New engines for '69 included a 155bhp 250cu in straight-six and two 351cu in V8s in 250 and 290bhp strengths. Ram Air 428s like this one came with a functional Shaker hood, which shook with the engine.

Left, and below: New for 1969 was the Mustang Mach 1. Available only as a "SportsRoof" fastback, it came with a long list of standard features which marked it out as the Mustang's sporty derivative. These included dual racing mirrors, flat black hood, and hood pins.

Right: The plush Deluxe Decor Group was standard interior on the Mach, while the 250bhp 351 was the standard engine. Mach 1s started at $3,122.

Classic Profile: *1969 FORD MUSTANG BOSS 429*

As part of Ford's commitment to motor sports, the Boss 429 was developed to homologate the 429 engine for NASCAR racing. This very limited run of cars was built at Kar Kraft in Brighton, Michigan. SportsRoof Mustangs were delivered to undergo extensive suspension modifications to accept the larger, more powerful 429 engine. Only 857 Boss 429 Mustangs were built.

Right: The Boss 429 listed for $1,208 over the list price of a regular SportsRoof. Interior was standard Mach 1, but there the resemblance ended.

Below: Boss 429 Mustangs received upgraded engine oil cooler, larger sway bars, rear-mounted battery, and a close-ratio four-speed manual transmission.

BOSS 429

Right: The 325bhp 429 used four-bolt mains, forged steel connecting rods, and crank. Producing 410lb ft torque, Boss 429s could do quarter miles in 14 seconds @ 102.8mph and 0-60mph in 7.1 seconds. Gas mileage rarely hit double digits, but this was a race car.

SPECIFICATIONS

Engine	7,031cc/429cu in
Horsepower	375@5,200rpm
Top speed	118mph (190kph)
Wheelbase	108in (274cm)
Weight	3,560lb (1,614kg)
Sales	857

Top left, and right: The big news for the 1969 Shelby Mustangs was their new Ram Air induction system. A trio of very business-like looking air scoops now graced the even-longer-for-'69 fiberglass hood. Convertible as well as SportsRoof bodystyles were available, although Shelby Mustangs bore little resemblance to stock Mustangs. GT350s came with a 280bhp 351 Windsor engine with Cobra valve covers, and an aluminum intake manifold. Unique Shelby wheels wore E70x15 tires, and air scoops up front and on the rear quarter panels ensured brakes were adequately cooled. At almost 176in long the GT350 was not the agile racing car it had been.

Left: 1969 was the last year for the Shelby Mustangs. Some '69s were updated to '70 model year cars. Total production for '69-'70 Shelby Mustangs (including GT500s) was 3,153 cars. The GT350 SportsRoof listed at $4,434, the convertible at $4,753.

Right: 1969 was the penultimate year for the Shelby Mustangs. In many ways they had become more of a styling package rather than fulfilling the performance pedigree with which they had been so closely associated in the early days of the Shelby Mustangs. Still, they sold relatively well and made a final reappearance for the 1970 model year.

Left: Shelby GT500s were priced at $4,709 for the SportsRoof and $5,027 for the convertible. Total GT500 production for '69 was 3,485.

Above: GT500s used the 335bhp 428 CJ. The 0-60 in 6.6 seconds, and a top speed of 130mph were good for a car weighing 3,850lb.

Above: Plymouth had a hit on their hands with the runaway sales success of its budget racer—the Roadrunner. Ford's answer was to offer the Fairlane Cobra, which came standard with Ford's feisty 428 Cobra Jet V8.

Right: The Cobra Jet engine propelled the mid-size Fairlane to 60mph in just over 6 seconds and could do 14 seconds on the quarter mile. Regular Cobra Jet 428s were rated at 335bhp; Super Cobra Jets with ram air were rated at 360bhp.

Left: Stock versions of the car on sale to the public came with the 335bhp Cobra Jet 428 engine. However, the racing versions utilized 427cu in racing engines at the start of the season, switching to semi-hemi 429 engines later. The Talladegas did well on the ovals for Ford, raising the profile of Torino SportsRoofs generally and boosting sales.

Left: Torino Talladegas were made by Ford for the 1969 model year to compete in NASCAR racing. Like Chrysler with its winged cars, Ford had turned its attention to aerodynamics, and despite being based on the Torino SportsRoof, Talladegas had fared-in headlights, and a more aerodynamic grille.

Right: To qualify for NASCAR racing, Ford had to build at least 500 examples of the car for sale to the public. Around 754 cars were actually built, making the Talladega a very rare performance car indeed. Mercury division ran a similar car, based on the Mercury Montego and called the Cyclone Spoiler II.

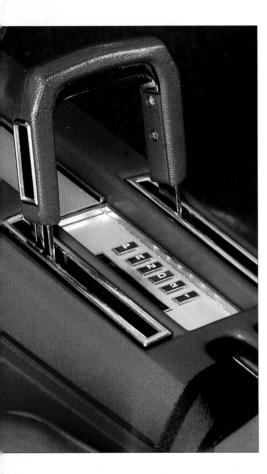

Right: Ford's exciting line of SportsRoof cars even included a full-size offering for 1969: the Galaxie XL GT 429. Pictured here with an Orange C-stripe, the GT 429 made up in visual impact what it lacked in pure performance.

Above: Ford's 429cu in V8 may have been a big engine, but the Galaxie was a big, heavy car and despite the GT moniker, it struggled to keep up with its Fairlane and Mustang GT stablemates.

Left : A sporty-look console held not only "shopping-basket" type automatic transmission shifter, but also belt holders.

Classic Profile: *1970 FORD MUSTANG MACH 1*

The Mach 1 was all about sporty looks. To this end, spoilers, striping and air scoops were in abundance, and made for an aggressively handsome-looking car. However, the Mach 1's appeal was more than skin deep. Fitted with the 351 Cleveland engine, it was a well-balanced package, offering better handling than the nose-heavy big-block versions. The 300bhp 351 might not have the grunt of a 428, but there was plenty of power, and the tighter handling package made up for any shortcomings in horsepower.

Left: For many, the 1970 Mustang's relatively compact dimensions were the last "proper" Mustangs before they got really big in the 1971 model year. The list price for Mach 1s was $3,271.

SPECIFICATIONS

Engine	5,752cc/351cu in
Horsepower	300@5,400rpm
Top speed	125mph (201kph)
Wheelbase	108in (274cm)
Weight	3,520lb (1,596kg)
Sales	40,970

Left: Mach 1 buyers got all the obvious styling goodies externally, like rear-window louvered sports slats, but inside they also benefited from the Mustang's deluxe bucket seats, and twin cockpit dash. Competition suspension, E70-15 tires, and color-keyed racing mirrors nicely rounded off the Mach 1 package.

Above: The four-barrel 351cu in V8 develops 300bhp @ 5,400rpm and 380lb ft of torque. It could achieve 0-60mph in 8.3 seconds, while quarter-mile times over 16 seconds @ 88mph were recorded. Perhaps not the fastest, but certainly one of the more agile Mustangs of the time.

Left: Developed for SCCA Trans Am racing, the 1970 Boss 302 Mustang is probably the ultimate muscle car that handles as well. Ford made sure the car could turn corners, and was powerful, too. The Boss 302 was a relatively light car at about 3,415lb, hence with its high-performance engine benefited from an excellent power-to-weight ratio.

Right: The Boss 302 listed at a base price of $3,720, almost $1,000 more than the cheapest Mustang. However, buyers got a car which was more or less ready to race off the showroom floor, including quick ratio steering, competition suspension, E70x15 fiberglass belted tires, front disc-brakes, and four-speed manual transmission.

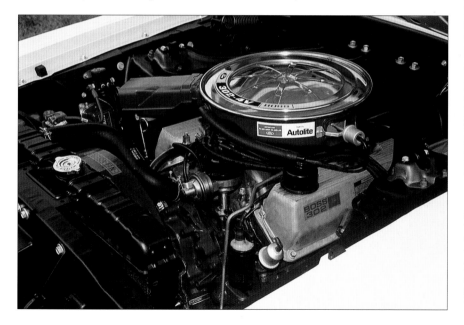

Left: Power comes from a 302cu in V8 rated at 290bhp @ 5,800rpm and 290lb ft of torque @ 4,300rpm. The Boss 302 was an impressive performer, not only in terms of handling but in straight-line performance. On the drag strip it could cover the quarter-mile in 15.8 seconds @ 90mph and reach 60mph in 6.5 seconds. Top speed was around 118 mph.

Right: This Grabber Blue Mustang Boss 302 was the closest thing to a factory production race car in 1970. Again, Ford had racing in mind when it developed the Boss 302. In this package, which cost a hefty $3,720 (regular Mustangs started at $2,721), buyers got four-speed manual transmission with Hurst shifter, 11in front disc-brakes, competition suspension, limited-slip differential, front spoiler and rear aerofoil, and F60x15 tires. A shaker hood scoop as seen here was optional. The motoring press of the time was almost universal in its praise for the Boss 302's excellent handling characteristics.

Left: The 302 engine produced 290bhp @ 5,800rpm and 290lb ft of torque. The '70 Boss 302s could do 0-60mph in 6.5 seconds and the quarter mile in under 15 seconds @ 97mph. Some 7,013 Boss 302s found buyers in 1970 out of a Mustang production of 190,727 cars.

Classic Profile: *1970 FORD MUSTANG BOSS 429*

The purpose of the Boss 429 was to clean up in NASCAR racing. Success in racing translated into great PR for Ford as a whole, although the Boss 429s, which were still being assembled by Kar Kraft, proved expensive. The cars sold for around $4,000, but it's believed they actually cost far more to build and Ford lost money on each car sold.
Nevertheless, they were great image-builders for Ford.

This 1970 Grabber Blue Boss 429 came with these handsome chrome Magnum 500 wheels.

SPECIFICATIONS

Engine	7,031cc/429cu in
Horsepower	375bhp@5,200rpm
Top speed	118mph (190kph)
Wheelbase	108in (274cm)
Weight	3,400lb (1,542kg)
Sales	499

Left: Demand for Boss 429 was high following their success in NASCAR. However, only 499 were built for 1970.

BOSS 429

Above: The 429 was an awesome engine, which was rated at 375bhp and 450lb ft of torque. The 0-60mph was achieved in around 7 seconds, and quarter miles in 14 seconds @ 103mph.

Left: Despite weighing almost 3,500lb, the Boss 429 enjoyed an excellent power to weight ratio, and Kar Kraft could barely build 'em fast enough.

Left: In its final incarnation, the Shelby Mustangs were a shadow of their former self. Like the Mustang itself, they had grown disproportionately large, losing that sports car agility which had made them so attractive as America's first true sports car.

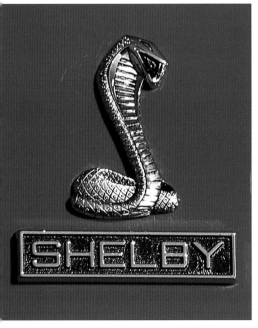

Left: 1970 Shelby Mustangs were virtually identical to the '69s. Indeed, many sources say they were surplus '69s which were unsold and which had their VINs "updated" to reflect 1970 model year.

Above: Along with the 335bhp 428 CJ engine, Shelby GT500 buyers got the Mustang's Deluxe Interior, as well as four-speed manual transmission. Only 601 Shelby Mustangs were sold in 1970, of which 286 were GT500s.

Right: Torinos were restyled for 1969, gaining almost 2ft in length, though still top of the tree was the Torino Cobra. Standard was the 360bhp 429, with the 370bhp Cobra 429 or the Cobra Jet Ram Air optional. Buyers got a four-speed manual transmission with Hurst shifter, F70-14 Wide Oval tires, blacked out hood, and staggered shocks.

Left: Ford built 7,675 Torino Cobras for the '69 model year. Starting price was $3,270. The 428 Cobra Jet was no longer available.

Above: This particular Torino Cobra has a shaker hood scoop which pokes through the hood and "shakes" with the engine, hence the name.

Left: This 1970 Ford Torino Cobra was one of three special cars built by Tasca Ford. For 1970, Torino Cobras came fitted with a base four-barrel 360bhp version of the 429, however buyers could opt for a 370bhp Cobra 429 or Cobra Jet Ram Air 429. Ford sold 7,675 Torino Cobras for 1970.

Above: The Torino had grown in almost every dimension for the 1970 model year and was priced at $3,270. Buyers got staggered shocks, competition suspension, a four-speed manual transmission with a Hurst shifter, blacked out hood, and F70x14 wide oval tires. This example has a Shaker hood.

Left: The Mustang underwent a massive restyle for 1971, and was now bigger, and heavier than ever. Wheelbase was finally extended to 109in, while overall length grew to 189.5in. The Muscle car era was drawing to an end, and the only Boss Mustang available was the Boss 351, which used the 330bhp 351cu in engine. Boss 351s came with four-speed manual transmission, and a 3.91:1 rear axle with Traction-Lok. Power front disc-brakes and competition suspension were also part of the package, as was a Ram Air induction system. Ford sold 1,806 Boss 351s, which were priced around $4,124.

Right: The Boss 351 now weighed 3,860lb. It may not have been as agile as its forebears, but it was still fast. Testers reported quarter-mile times in the 14 second range at over 100mph, and 0-60mph times in around 6 seconds, not bad for a car nudging almost 4,000lb.

Classic Profile: *1971 FORD MUSTANG MACH 1*

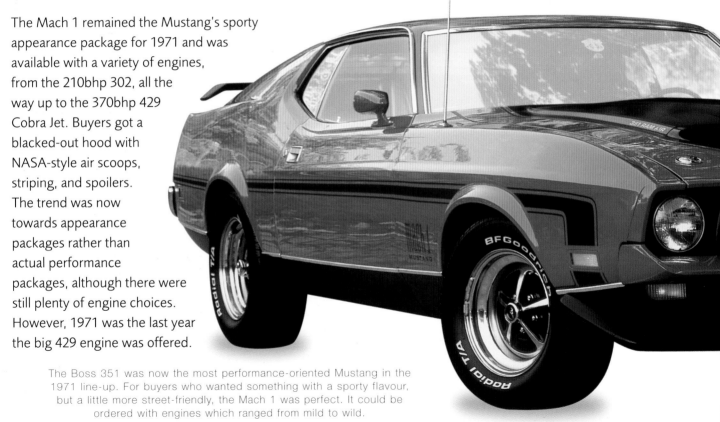

The Mach 1 remained the Mustang's sporty appearance package for 1971 and was available with a variety of engines, from the 210bhp 302, all the way up to the 370bhp 429 Cobra Jet. Buyers got a blacked-out hood with NASA-style air scoops, striping, and spoilers. The trend was now towards appearance packages rather than actual performance packages, although there were still plenty of engine choices. However, 1971 was the last year the big 429 engine was offered.

The Boss 351 was now the most performance-oriented Mustang in the 1971 line-up. For buyers who wanted something with a sporty flavour, but a little more street-friendly, the Mach 1 was perfect. It could be ordered with engines which ranged from mild to wild.

SPECIFICATIONS

Engine	5,752cc/351cu in
Horsepower	285bhp@5,400rpm
Top speed	116mph (187kph)
Wheelbase	109in (276cm)
Weight	3,220lb (1,460kg)
Sales	36,499

Right: A honeycomb grille with driving lights, color-keyed mirrors, and bumpers, and black or argent lower bodysides came as part of the Mach 1 package.

Below right: This Mach 1 is fitted with the four-barrel Cleveland 351, which turned out 285bhp @ 5,400rpm. Buyers could also opt for the Cobra Jet 429 or the Super Cobra Jet 429 with Ram Air Induction.

Far right: Mach 1s came with a Sports Interior, which included knitted vinyl seats, electric clock, and wood applique.

Right: Fitted with a 370bhp 429 Cobra Jet with Ram Air, Mach 1s like this could do 0-60mph in under 7 seconds.

Below: Despite weighing in at 3,805lb, the Mach 1 was still pretty quick, capable of doing the quarter mile in under 15 seconds @ 96mph.

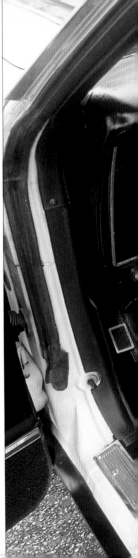

Left: The 1972 Mustangs differed little from the '71s. Sales dropped again to 125,093 cars. Only 27,675 Mach 1s found buyers. There was no big-block engine option, the hottest now being a high-output 351 which made a brief appearance.

Above: As performance options were watered down, so Ford had to come up with other ways of marketing their cars. This was principally done with the use of appearance packages. Slowly, but surely, the muscle car was being emasculated.

CLASSIC MARQUES

MERCURY

9

1970 Mercury Cougar Eliminator

Right: The Comet Cyclone was Mercury's hot offering for 1965. Weighing 2,994lb and priced at $2,625, Mercury sold 12,347 Cyclones in '65.

Left, and below: Cyclones came with a 200bhp 289cu in V8, plus bucket seats, console, and tachometer. It was a hot performer, with 0-60 in under 9 seconds and quarter-mile times under 17.

Left, and below: Mercury's handsome intermediate changed little from 1967, following its extensive restyle in '66. The Comet Cyclone GT remained the hot one in Mercury's line-up, with a four-barrel 390cu in V8 rated at 320bhp and 427lb ft of torque. Three-speed manual transmission was standard, with a four-speed available or Merc-O-Matic automatic.

Left: A very small number of Mercury Comet Cyclones were fitted with Ford's highly strung 410bhp 427 engine. It was a screamer up the strip, but around town could be a handful!

Classic Profile: *1969 CYCLONE CALE YARBOROUGH*

The use of so called "signature" models was the big marketing story of the '60s, and what better way to publicize your racing successes than naming a model after one of your most famous drivers: Cale Yarborough. Yarborough raced for Lincoln-Mercury in the SCCA Trans-Am series, Dan Gurney also gave his name to a special edition Cyclone, too. Today these signature series cars are highly prized by collectors and fetch premium prices over regular non-signature models.

Left, and right: Power for the Cyclone II came from a 290bhp four-barrel Windsor 351. Buyers also got FMX Cruise-O-Matic Transmission and 3.25:1 Traction-Lok gears.

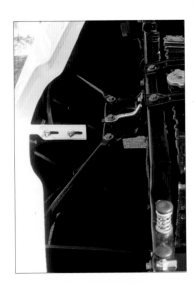

Below: Like Ford's Torino Talladegas, Cyclone Spoiler IIs were designed to be totally aerodynamic.

SPECIFICATIONS

Engine	5,752cc/351cu in
Horsepower	290@5,200rpm
Wheelbase	116in (294cm)
Weight	3,273lb (1,484kg)
Sales	300 (both)

The Cale Yarborough Cyclone Spoiler IIs enjoyed special striping, badging, and a rear spoiler. A total of 519 Cyclone Spoiler IIs were built in '69.

Above, and right: Cyclone Spoiler IIs came with a four-barrel 351cu in V8. Two trim packages were available, named after racers Dan Gurney and Cale Yarborough.

Left: The 1969 Cyclone Spoiler IIs were designed with NASCAR racing in mind. Aerodynamics was the hot ticket and manufacturers were trying everything to make their cars slip-streamed, from spoilers to flush grilles.

Above: Mercury produced an especially hot version of the Cougar for 1969—the Cougar Eliminator. It was Mercury's answer to the Boss 302 and the Mach 1. Base engine was the 290bhp 351, but buyers could order a number of other engines, including the 428 Cobra Jet.

Right: Ford's 428cu in Cobra Jet produced 335bhp, reaching the quarter mile in just 14 seconds. The Eliminator package included an oil cooler with the 428, staggered shocks, tachometer, power front-disc brakes, heavy duty suspension, and various transmission choices. Only around 500 Eliminators were built.

Above: Engine options for the 1970 Mercury Cougar Eliminator were extensive and included the Boss 302 engine, as seen here, as well as a 375bhp Boss 429 package, which included Ram Air; a 300bhp 351 came as standard, however.

Right: Only minor styling changes differentiated the 1970 Mercury Cougars from the '69s. The Eliminator returned for the final time, with special striping, hood scoop, and rear deck spoiler to mark it out as the Cougar's performance special.

Left: 1970 Cyclone Spoilers continued in the quest for greater aerodynamics, as NASCAR competition from Dodge's Daytonas and Plymouth's Superbird was making things tough for Ford.

Far left, and below: Spoilers came with a 370bhp Ram Air 429 engine and were listed at $3,530. Mercury sold 1,631 Cyclone Spoilers, which for 1970 had grown by almost 7in. Regular Cyclones were available with either the 370bhp Cobra Jet or 375bhp Super Cobra Jet engines. The Cyclone Spoiler would make one final appearance in '71.

CYCLONE SPOILER

Above: The 1971 Cougar XR7 was the more luxurious model in the Cougar line-up. Buyers got full instrumentation, a cherrywood applique dash, and leather seat facings. For '71 the Cougar grew and lost its hide-away headlights. It remained a handsome car.

Left: A non-functional hoodscoop was available to Cougar buyers at extra cost, however when Ram Air induction was ordered with the 370bhp 429 engine. The air cleaner is joined to the hoodscoop via a rubber seal around its rim, as seen here.

Right: Cougars were available with either 240bhp or 285bhp versions of the 351cu in or for those interested in even more power, a 370bhp 429cu in V8. A 429-powered Cougar could turn in 14.64 second quarter-mile times at almost 100mph.

INDEPENDENTS

1970 AMC Rebel Machine

10

Classic Profile: *1969 AMC HURST SC/RAMBLER 'A'*

Everyone wanted a slice of the lucrative muscle car market, and AMC were no exception to this rule. One of the most original and unconventional muscle cars of the era was the Hurst SC/Rambler. Based on the popular Rambler Rogue, AMC stuffed its biggest engine under the hood (a 325bhp 390cu in V8), and slapped on some eye-scorching paint and a home-made looking hood scoop. It was cheap and cheerful, but highly effective, and the SC/Rambler, despite its oddball looks, was a serious contender on the drag strip.

SPECIFICATIONS

Engine	6,392cc/390cu in
Horsepower	315bhp@4,600rpm
Top speed	114mph (183kph)
Wheelbase	106in (269cm)
Weight	2,988lb (1,355kg)
Sales	1,512

Right: Priced at under $3,000 ($2,998), the SC/Rambler offered a lot for a very reasonable price. The only option was a $61 AM radio. Interiors featured bucket seats, and wood-rimmed steering wheel, plus an aftermarket tachometer strapped to the steering column.

Right: AMC's 390 was quite a powerhouse when ordered in the diminutive SC/Rambler—0-60mph came up in 6.3 seconds and it could cover the quarter mile in 14.7 seconds @ 96.3mph. It might look funny, but it was fast!

Right: Buyers got a Borg-Warner four-speed manual transmission with Hurst shifter, Twin Grip limited-slip differential, dual exhaust, heavy duty cooling system, and heavy duty brakes, including discs on the front. Much of this hardware was lifted wholesale from AMC's AMX.

Above: For 1969 AMC offered the Big Bad Javelins like this one in Big Bad Blue. These had fenders painted the same color as the body, plus a close-ratio four-speed Hurst shifter, spoiler, Twin-Grip differential, power front disc-brakes, and E70x14 Goodyear Polyglass Red Line tires. Big Bad Javelins also came in eye-scorching green and orange.

Right: The 1969 AMC Javelin was offered with a variety of engines, starting with the 145bhp 232cu in straight six, up to a big 315bhp 390cu in V8. Buyers could also select from four-speed manual or automatic transmission. An upmarket version called the Javelin SST offered extra chrome, special trim, and bucket seats.

Right: AMC sold over 40,000 Javelins for the '69 model year, which meant they weren't much of a sales threat to Ford or GM, which sold almost 300,000 Mustangs and 230,000 Camaros respectively.

Above: The AMX was based on a shortened version of the Javelin and was a two-seater introduced in 1968. With its short 97in wheelbase, the AMX was one of the best handling cars of its time and was relatively light too, meaning excellent quarter mile times: 10.73 @ 128 in super stock form.

Right: AMC loaded the AMX with performance goodies, such as heavy-duty suspension, sway bar, and shocks. The standard engine in 1970 was the 290bhp 390cu in V8, however sales fell to an all time low of 4,116 units and AMC decided to discontinue the AMX.

Below: Hood-mounted tachometers were a popular feature on late-'60s, early-'70s muscle cars. Machine buyers also got a Ram Air induction set-up, heavy-duty shocks, and springs, front and rear sway bars, and four-speed close ratio manual transmission with a Hurst shifter.

Far left: Where AMC had saved on trim and appearance goodies—but not with the wheels—they went to town in terms of performance hardware, offering their biggest 390cu in engine, which was rated at 340bhp and which could return quarter mile times of 14.4 seconds @ 98mph. Priced at $3,475, AMC sold relatively few machines, selling only 2,326 in 1970.

Above: AMC had acquired a reputation for the ability to create eye-catching, high performance machines at a knock-down price. The Rebel Machine was a classic example. Based on AMC's relatively mundane Rebel, the Machine boasted a flamboyant red, white and blue paint scheme, and a massive shoebox-like hood scoop.

INDEX